AROUND CHINA IN 300 DAYS
A journey through 30 cities and towns

Taddeo Bwambale Nyondo

AROUND CHINA IN 300 DAYS

A journey through 30 cities and towns

Copyright © 2017 by African Centre for Literary Arts

ISBN: 978-9970-9708-0-3

Photos by Taddeo Bwambale Nyondo

Designed by Elias Muhwezi

Address

African Centre for Literary Arts

P.O BOX 34481, Kampala

Telephone: +256 312 517 225

CONTENTS

DEDICATION

To my beloved: Elizabeth and Moses.

ACKNOWLEDGEMENT

Thank you, Barbara Kaija, for this book would never have been born, were it not for your confidence in my abilities.

Special thanks to the China-Africa Press Centre and the Embassy of the People's Republic of China in Uganda for making my stay in China a memorable experience. Appreciation to *Vision Group* for giving me time to gather new knowledge.

To my family, friends and colleagues who have been with me throughout the arduous journey of preparing this book; sincere thanks to you: Sam, Joe, Elias and all those I have not mentioned.

Above all, I thank God, who makes all things possible!

INTRODUCTION

What do you see in a road, a bridge or railway line? Some will see a path, skirting across endless terrain. The Chinese see a path to grow rich: a connection to the world. That is exactly what you see when you travel across the four corners of China.

I arrive in Beijing towards the end of February, a time when winter is just receding. For someone who has lived all my life in the tropics (Uganda), I must brace myself for so much more.

A very gracious man (Pan Xiaoguang) comes to receive me at Beijing Capital International Airport. He turns out to be one of the leaders of the programme for which I have been invited. If that alone is not humbling.

I catch a glimpse of the gleaming skyline as we drive about 30km from the airport to the heart of Beijing. The world here is quite different. So many skyscrapers. Welcome to China.

I spend my first few days in China trying to make sense of Beijing. Life here is pretty fast. People walk and talk quite fast. Maybe it's the cold. Or maybe it's their culture. The people I come across are generally warm and friendly. They drink tea all the time. A cab driver will have a flask with tea in the trunk or next to the dashboard. In the offices, meetings start with a cup of tea. What's much more, it's tea without sugar. What's much more, it's tea without sugar. There is even a place where people go to celebrate a tea culture dating back 4,000 years.

For the next few days I get time to move about to see more of Beijing, a city of relative contrasts - where the ancient past meets the modern times. Many leading international brands spread across every street. High-end shopping malls stand next to ancient architectural landmarks and historical sites, in some form of mutual solitude.

Western coffee shops and restaurant chains (Starbucks, Burger King, KFC or McDonald's) sit next to traditional Chinese restaurants.

For a first time visitor, it is hard to believe you are in a developing country. Beijing has as much or even more of what you would find in any of the world's well-known capitals.

The last days of February herald not only the dying weeks of winter, but also the start of China's busiest political season. Two of the most watched political meetings take place around this time.

One of these is a conference of the Chinese People's Political Consultative Conference (CPPCC), the country's top political advisory body. Days later, the National People's Congress (NPC) - the legislative assembly - will also meet to evaluate government work performance for the year ended.

At least 600,000 CPPCC members and the NPC's 3,000 delegates will sit for two weeks inside an iconic mansion at the edge of Tiananmen Square and known as the 'Great Hall of the People.'

In full glare of clicking cameras, members of the political advisory body and the legislature stroll into the building with some sort of fanfare. We brave the biting cold, thousands of us journalists, to get into the building.

For the next two weeks, politics and the economy dominate discussion. The world watches keenly what comes out of China, from growth figures to new development plans and forecasts.

For 2016, we are told that for the first time in almost thirty years, China's economy is slowing down, but under control. World media jumps into a frenzy.

It is also revealed that 14 million jobs were created, about 14.4 million taken out of poverty and an average 12,000 new businesses created daily during the past year.

Meanwhile, a new five-year plan targeting to make every Chinese national moderately prosperous by 2020 is scrutinized and approved by delegates. It speaks of the search for new engines of growth and China's push from manufacturing and coal production. It paints a shift to services, technology, innovation and clean energy. President Xi Jinping attends the two sessions and sits there as a participant. He will have to raise his hand like every other delegate if he wants to make a suggestion.

At the end of the two sessions, the delegates hand over proposals to government and return to their duties. They will meet again to review progress on government work after 12 months.

Such has been the model of political representation in China under the Communist Party of China (CPC), which has been at the helm of power since 1949. The country ascribes to 'Socialism' but with Chinese characteristics as the guiding political philosophy. Socialism advocates for collective or public ownership of means of production, unlike the capitalist model which encourages private ownership of capital and means of production.

With the fall of the Berlin Wall in the late 1980s, the economies in communist Europe crumbled under the weight of new shifts. China stuck to the communist ideology but refined it to suit domestic circumstances.

China has risen from a large, poor country to the world's second largest economy in a space of 30 years using a unique approach to development. The country underwent rapid industrialization and maintained exceptionally high growth rates between the late 1960s and 1990s. People talk about the 'China Miracle,' through which more than 660 million people have come out of poverty in one generation. For the ordinary Chinese people here, wages are rising, the standard of living is improving and income inequality is declining.

China's turning point is widely traced to the 'reform and opening up' era in the late 1970s under paramount leader, Deng Xiaoping. The pith of the reform was attracting foreign investment from the US, Europe, Japan and South Korea, which were more advanced in terms of economy and technology.

China's rapid rise from a large, poor country to the world's second largest economy in a space of 30 years has left scholars and researchers questioning age-old development models. At first it was the Four Asian Tigers or Asian Dragons (Hong Kong, Singapore, South Korea and Taiwan), countries that underwent rapid industrialization and maintained exceptionally high growth rates between the early 1960s and 1990s. Today, people talk about the 'China Miracle,' a story about the transformation of mainland China. Over 660 million people have been lifted out of poverty in one generation. For the ordinary people here, wages are rising, the standard of living is rising and income inequality is declining.

China's turning point is widely traced to the 'reform and opening up' era in the late 1970s under Deng Xiaoping. The pith of the reform was attracting foreign investment from the US, Europe, Japan and South Korea, which were already advanced in terms of economy and technology.

By the late 1990s, Chinese enterprises had acquired the technology, capital and infrastructure to produce extensively, becoming the world's largest industrial base. Massive investment in infrastructure over the past three decades has turned China, one of the most geographically challenged countries on the planet, into one of the most interconnected regions on the planet. An extensive network of expressways, bridges and tunnels crisscrosses vast terrain, linking erstwhile reclusive towns and cities into thriving development hubs.

Nowhere is this transformation more visible than deep in the provinces, regions, cities and towns, where the power of ambition and hard work is shifting the tide. It's time to venture out of Beijing to one of the provinces where tourism and culture are transforming an ancient island into a modern treasure.

xii

HAINAN

A five-hour flight from Beijing takes us far south to Hainan, a warm, temperate province. It is the smallest and southernmost province of China, located on the edge of the South China Sea.

The blend of tropical climate and coastal scenery has made Hainan one of China's most popular travel destinations for tourists seeking more than just respite from the biting winter. Hainan consists of over two hundred islands scattered among three archipelagos off the southern coast. It is also the largest Special Economic Zone established by Chinese leader Deng Xiaoping in the late 1980s. So, what do you see when you get to Hainan?

Haikou City

Right from Haikou Meilan International Airport, what you find is a sudden change in culture – from Bermuda shirts and shorts to warm, sunny weather. This city is home to about three million residents, tucked in a well-built up area across four urban districts. Here is a city described as the 'Garden City of China,' and there's good reason for that. Rows and rows of coconut trees line the streets of Haikou, giving it a distinct identity.

Haikou City has a long history as an important trade hub in Asia, dating back to the Song and Yuan dynasties (960 and 1368). The city was formerly a part of Guangdong province, and in the 13th century, it served as a military post under the Ming dynasty (1368–1644). Numerous relics of this ancient past are visible landmarks and important tourist attractions in this city.

We travel across Hainan with the help of Gan Dafan, a famous tour guide who has lived much of his life in the southern province. He prefers to be called 'Sunny.'

The 42-year-old native knows each of Hainan Island's cities so well and has seen rapid changes in the lives of the region's more than nine million inhabitants.

But it is perhaps his unusual skill at storytelling, more than his breadth of knowledge about the island, that has made him famous around the pristine island. Beyond simply describing places, Sunny sings for tourists and entertains them with folktales during bus trips along the journey. His admirable camaraderie with strangers and his use of comedy to amuse tourists has left him with more friends than just guests.

He grew up in Hainan's Wenchang City, where he spent much of his youth travelling around the province. After leaving school he found work at a local tour company and he has never looked back.

In his hometown, Gafan recalls that life was so hard that sometimes there wasn't enough food in the house to eat. The coconuts he and his peers saw purely as food now decorate the streets of Haikou.

"Sometimes we would sneak into people's gardens to steal coconuts. One time, the owner of one garden set his dogs upon us," he narrates, before breaking into song once more.

Today, skyscrapers and commercial properties sit on much of the land in his hometown where coconut trees used to be in abundance. Shiny tourist buses in different colours ply city routes on neat paved roads. Upper class theatres and shopping malls are spread all over major suburbs of Haikou. The standard of living here has greatly improved, observes Gafan.

"In ancient times, this island was known as the end of the world. Criminals and exiles were sent here as punishment," he explains, before breaking into an ancient song. Today, people go to Hainan by their own volition, drawn to the island by its enchanting landmarks.

Apart from tourism, the province is home to some of the most successful home-grown companies. Take for instance, Hainan Airlines (HNA Group), a \$145b conglomerate that started out as a small regional airline 20 years ago. HNA Group is now one of the country's leading private enterprises, with interests in hotels, finance, advertising and property development. Started at the height of China's economic reform in 1993, HNA has expanded globally with huge stakes in such big brands as Hilton Hotels and Swissport, as well as Germany's Deutsche Bank where it is now the largest investor.

The city of Haikou is also home to Yingli, a private company that is now the world's largest producer of solar panels. One out of every ten solar panels sold across the world comes out of this production plant. One of Yingli's research areas is about a type of solar modules designed to power a car. Although the idea is years away from fruition, ambition and innovation seem boundless in the city of Haikou.

Wanning City

We take a bus to Wanning, a county-level city in the southeast of Hainan. Here lies a city teeming with pristine beaches and several five-star hotels. Wanning is connected to the rest of Hainan via modern public transportation platforms, including a vibrant inter-city railway network. Famous for its tropical scenery, this city is a perfect get-away for tourists from near and far. Tourism is clearly the backbone of the economy in this region.

Besides tourism, Wanning is an agricultural hub, one of China's leading producers of fruits, coffee, black pepper, rubber, rice and sugarcane. With access to the sea, this southern part of China is a leading exporter of agricultural products both for the domestic market and overseas.

To understand the scale of China's investment in agricultural research, we take a trip to the Xinlong Tropical Botanical Garden, one of the most popular tourist attractions in Wanning City.

Sitting on an area of about 42 hectares and surrounded by mountains in the southeast of Hainan, the botanical garden is home to China's biggest inventory of tropical plant species.

Founded in 1957 as a non-profit research institute under China's ministry of agriculture, the facility is the base for collecting and preserving tropical crops and plants from within China and overseas.

The expansive facility comprises of different zones including a plant-viewing area, experiment and demonstration area, research and development area, planting area and ecological leisure park. The variety of tropical plants here includes beverage and aromatic crops, tropical fruit trees, tree species, ornamental and medicinal and aquatic plants, endangered plants and vegetable crops.

It has a collection of over 4,000 varieties of plants and crops, including bananas, jackfruit, coffee, tea, pepper, vanilla, cocoa and cinnamon.

Some of the rare plant species grown here were collected from Africa and parts of Asia. At the facility, the plants are grown, studied in detail and samples mass-produced to address some of China's farming needs.

The botanical garden has 120 employees, including 65 scientists, technicians and 23 university professors. Their task is simple: to conduct scientific studies that lead to improvement in agriculture production. The botanical garden is in many ways a quintessence of a development model that highlights an interplay between agriculture, science and tourism.

This, perhaps, explains why China, a country of 1.3 billion people, is able to feed itself without relying on food imports. Hainan is one of China's largest producers of tropical fruits and out-of-season vegetables. With the help of scientific research, value addition in agriculture generated $13 billion in 2015. Over the last five years, farmers' incomes have doubled, and so has per capita income, from $788 to $1625 in 2015.

Hundreds of people visit the facility every day, drawn to it by the large profile of rare tropical plant species. Radiant flowers sprout and spread across flourishing green spaces, creating a harmonious scenic beauty of nature. Visitors to this park can choose to either walk or take a ride in a cart. There is also chance for visitors to try out the local coffee and tea varieties grown in the garden. There's also a supermarket and several stalls where visitors can buy snacks, beverages and spices – all produced at this botanical park.

Sanya City

A high-speed train ride from Wanning gets us to our next stop: the enchanting city of Sanya, located in the southernmost part of Hainan Island. Much more like Wanning, Sanya is renowned for its tropical climate and numerous tourist sites. In the city of about a million people, more than 100 hotels and resorts have sprung up in recent years. Busloads of tourists flock to this city every day. For some visitors, it's all about the alluring natural attractions and scenery. Yet still, others come here to relive China's ancient past tucked in the vast forest mountains, an area where two ethnic minority communities have dwelt and thrived for centuries.

One such treasure trove in Sanya is the Binglanggu Heritage Park, a cultural theme park that draws its name from the local ethnic minority villages and the countless betel trees that extend several kilometers along the valley.

The park sits on 333 hectares and gives visitors a snapshot into ancient life of the Li and Miao ethnic communities and their vast intangible cultural heritage village.

At the start of the tour around the expansive park, visitors get a feel of the native culture of the Li and Miao people through a live show. Tasty betel nuts and snacks are aplenty around the park.

Audiences are treated to a musical performance featuring a bamboo dance, costumes show and ancient traditional practices of rice husking, betel-nut picking, tree climbing and fish stabbing.

Against a backdrop of beautiful tropical natural scenery, Binlanggu is a 'museum' of rich ancient history, offering visitors insight into a native way of life dating back more than 100 years.

The park is regarded a 'living fossil of Hainan ethnic culture' and was declared a national intangible cultural heritage centre by the Chinese government.

The traditional spinning, dyeing, weaving and embroidery techniques of the Li ethnic group, shown at the park, are listed as intangible cultural heritage in need of urgent safeguarding by UNESCO.

Built in 1998, Binlanggu is a tourism destination devoted to the protection and promotion of the ancient ethnic culture of the Li people.

Spread across the park are preserved aboriginal huts depicting the simple lifestyle of the Li and Miao people, next to a museum of culture that exhibits cloth and other artifacts of the minorities.

Century-old granaries, ancient nose-flute musical instruments, pottery, coconut workshops and a tattoo museum dot around the captivating landscape. It is feared that the embroidered surface tattoo procedure of the Li ethnic group, exhibited inside the museum, will be extinct in ten years.

How did the Li and Miao people make wine from rice and corn? Visitors get a taste of wine and whisky made from the grains, using an ancient fermentation technique.

From ancient spider king medicine, alluring traditional attire, silverware and cuisine, Binlanggu Heritage Park is a quiet encyclopedia of human history.

One of the sculptures inside the museum depicts Huang Daopol (1245-1330), a cotton textile expert who visited the area during the Yuan Dynasty from present-day Xuhui district in Shanghai. She is widely credited with popularizing the art of spinning and weaving which she learnt from the Li and Miao, which in turn catapulted China's textile industry in later years.

Binlanggu is one of China's top ten filming locations in China. Its beautiful landscape has turned it into a popular filming location for movies, TV series and reality shows.

At the end of the sprawling heritage is the Zhong Liao Village, a modern village with housing facilities built for the ethnic minorities. The natives here are connected to urban areas through a network of neat roads and a one-stop centre that provides e-government services and free Wi-Fi.

Our last stop in the city of Sanya is at the famous Romance Park, a large cultural tourism theme park that hosts about half a million tourists every year. Acrobatics, dance, art, poetry and dance routines showcase the colorful multicultural history of Sanya City.

A large part of the performances highlights important episodes in Chinese history or her interaction with the outside world. An ancient Sanya is recreated with the aid of holographic special effects, modern technology and science fiction with myths, legends, history and culture.

The seats slide sideways, making room for performers to get across on a floating glass floor. Dancers slide above our heads on suspended platforms. Outside the theatre, dozens of temples court visitors with the fragrance from burning incense sticks and a subtle charm for blessings. Love is, evidently, one of the blessings sought from the gods tonight. Souvenir shops scream for attention in all directions. There goes Sanya, once a remote settlement known as "the end of the sky and ocean" but today a thriving tourist destination.

Boao Town

Our final tour of Hainan leads us to Boao, a thriving coastal town that was once just a rural fishing village. The town hosts the Boao Forum for Asia (BFA), a high-level meeting of leaders from government, business and academia in Asia and beyond.

Those who visit Boao come face to face with its string of luxury hotels and tourist facilities that draw many overseas Chinese to the coastal town every day.

Boao is an inter-connected town linked to neighbouring cities by shuttle buses, bullet train and taxis. It takes about two hours to get to Boao from Sanya and about an hour Haikou.

The town is surrounded by beautiful natural scenery that includes mountains and sits at the mouth of the Wanquan River where it discharges into the South China Sea.

Our journey through Hainan has come to an end. It's time to pack our bags and bid farewell to Sunny, our tour guide. He will stay behind in this paradise and sing the story of her past and present. Sunny will try to keep the legend alive.

PICTORIAL

HAIKOU ▸▸

An aerial view of Haikou

Coconut trees in Haikou

The people of Haikou are friendly

The writer poses for a photo with statues in Haikou

WANNING ▸▸

Entertainers at the Xinlong Botanical Garden in Wanning City, Hainan Province

SANYA ▸▸

Performance relives ancient life of Li and Mia ethnic minorities in Sanya

BOAO ▸▸

Boao Forum is held against the backdrop of Wanquan River and the South China Sea

Greenery around Boao, a coastal town that has transformed from a rural fishing village

Boao has a well-laid out transport system

Gan Dafan, a tour guide in Hainan sings for tourists on the bus

JIANGSU

Next up, we head to the province of Jiangsu, located in the middle of China's east coast and the Yangtze River Delta. Home to about 80 million people, Jiangsu is one of the regions with the highest population density in China. The province borders Shanghai and Zhejiang to the south, Anhui to the west and Shandong to the north. It is endowed with a coastline of over 1,000 kilometers along the Yellow Sea and the Yangtze River, the longest river in China, which passes through the province in the south.

Jiangsu is one of the most prosperous and dynamic economies of China, with a GDP for 2015 exceeding $1 trillion and making it China's second largest economic power base after Guangdong Province.

Jiangsu has a sprawling industrial base covering electronics, metals, outsourcing services, IT, automotive, biotechnology, petrochemical, pharmaceutical and industrial machinery. Years of reform in key areas of the economy such as taxation, e-commerce, agriculture and environment have paid off. Half of the revenue generated by the province comes from the private sector, while technology and culture are becoming major drivers of economic development.

Nanjing City

When you drive through Nanjing, the capital of Jiangsu Province, one of the landmarks that will catch your eye is the ancient city wall. Held together by layers of bricks, granite and limestone that still stand today, the wall was designed by Emperor Zhu Yuanzhang, who founded the Ming Dynasty (1368–1644) and established Nanjing as the capital 600 years ago. In the ancient days, the wall was used to keep out invaders. Today, it stands out as an attraction for many visitors. Rows of plane trees (also known as Nanjing phoenix trees) spread across some streets of Nanjing. The tree is the city's cultural and natural heritage.

Nanjing means 'South City' and remains one of the most important historical, political, commercial and cultural nerve centres of China.

Our first stop in Nanjing is at the home of Jiangsu Broadcasting Corporation (JSBC), the third largest television network in China. Established in 2001, the vibrant JSBC now runs 16 television channels, 11 radio stations, a newspaper and a magazine. JSBC also runs a film studio, cinemas, audiovisual press, newspapers, magazines, websites and a media school, raking in at least $2 billion every year.

This is besides content production, a web television portal, movie distribution business, animation and cable network. The building, and what goes on inside of it, says something about China's media growth and expansion in recent years.

Within 15 years, the multi-media corporation has transcended traditional mass media models by relying on a philosophy you won't find in a textbook.

We meet Ren Tong, JSBC Vice President and head of international outreach. Technology has been the driver of transformation in the media industry, he says.

In the era of smartphones and the internet, traditional mass media must be more agile to stay afloat, he suggests, rather than bemoan the tragedy of an era.

The JSBC Tower is a towering landmark in the heart of the city that speaks of power, reach and ambition. Inside the building lie modern television and production studios with state-of-the-art equipment.

The night is bright in Nanjing, but perhaps nowhere more than along the famous Qinhuai River. We take a ride on the river inside ornately-painted boats. Qinhuai is the biggest river in Nanjing and a tributary of the Yangtze River. For thousands of years, Qinhuai River nurtured the ancient city of Nanjing. In modern times, the river has become such an important tourist destination.

It turns out to be a charming experience as we turn and turn around ancient structures preserved for tourists to see. In the midst of this attraction is the Confucius Temple, an important symbol of culture and faith in this ancient city. Nanjing tea and snacks are served to tourists aboard the decorated boats to spice up the hour-long cruise, under an enchanting pall of darkness and light.

Scores of revelers wait patiently to take a ride on the boats. Some just walk around the streets that are littered with wine shops, tea houses, snack stalls and handicraft shops.

Cultural tourism is big business in China. The Chinese people have tapped into their history and culture to attract tourism. Day and night there will be some form of attraction that is certain to draw visitors from near and far.

We make a stop at the Nanjing Drum Tower Hospital, one of the earliest western medical facilities built in China. Set up in 1892, the 3,000-bed hospital is now one of the advanced hospitals in China.

Patients here can book or consult doctors electronically, with dozens of health specialists conducting complex procedures, including organ transplant. With three million outpatient visits and 90,000 patient admissions annually, it is one of the busiest anywhere.

But more than just a tower of health service delivery, the iconic hospital represents China's interaction with the world. For one, its founder, Dr. Edward William Macklin, was a Canadian missionary who helped treat the poor when he set foot in the area. Since 1964, Chinese medical teams from this hospital have been dispatched to health missions overseas, including in Africa. We meet Ji Jiangdong, who has worked in Zanzibar as an eye specialist, helping to restore sight to over 1,430 people through cataract surgery. His colleague, Sun Kewen, has helped set up the first endoscopy centre at Mnazi Mmoja Hospital in Tanzania.

Suzhou City

"Up above there is heaven; on earth below there is Suzhou and Hangzhou," is a popular ancient description for two of China's most beautiful cities. We travel by high-speed train to Suzhou, a city founded in 514 BC and holding more than 2,500 years of rich history.

Suzhou is located on the lower reaches of the Yangtze River, the third longest river in the world that remains of historical, economic and cultural significance to China.

The city's history and culture have been preserved through canals, stone bridges and pagodas that sit alongside modern architectural landmarks, creating a blend of old and new civilizations.

Decades of economic reforms started in the 1970s have turned Suzhou into one of the fastest-growing major cities in the world, with an economic growth rate averaging 14% over the past 25 years.

The city's proximity to Shanghai, and its thriving tourism and manufacturing power, have turned it into one of China's top foreign investment destinations.

Perhaps no better story illustrates the transformation of Suzhou than the story of Suzhou Industrial Park (SIP), now one of the world's leading industrial parks built on what was once a field of rice paddies.

Here is how industrial parks work: land is identified, zoned and linked by roads, telecommunication services, water supply and energy to make it self-supporting. With the numerous financial incentives, the selected area is thus positioned to attract investors (foreign investors mostly), who bring with them capital, technology and skills. The investments, in turn, create jobs, pay taxes and bring in the much-needed foreign currency. This is the model that has helped attract leading global brands to many parts of China.

When the late Chinese paramount leader Deng Xiaoping approached Singapore's then-senior minister, Lee Kuan Yew for development guidance in the 1990s, a joint project would blossom.

Two decades after its establishment in 1994, the 288 square-kilometre park is now home to clusters of advanced industries and a planned residential area that serves as a model for smart living.

Massive investment in infrastructure is evident across the expansive city. By the end of 2015, Suzhou had a paved road network of 13,239km, with over 550km of interconnecting expressways.

Over the last ten years, the park has grown by 30%, attracting over 5,000 foreign firms, including 300 of the Fortune 500 enterprises. The SIP has inspired at least nine new development zones in Suzhou.

Around the SIP, many home-grown businesses have taken notice. One such firm is Higer, a company manufacturing luxury buses. Futuristic technologies and designs for advanced models for urban transport are some of the ideas being tested at this thriving industrial hub: from self-driving buses to artificial intelligence. For instance, the bus company is working on a concept to produce electric and hydrogen-powered buses that are environmentally friendly.

The SIP model has transformed a rural area full of rice paddies three decades ago into a modern commercial and residential suburb. This is how a city of only 12 million residents generated over $147b in revenue in 2015 alone. There will be no better symbol of transformation of Suzhou than when the city inaugurates the tallest building in China (730 metres high) in a few months to come.

We visit one of the companies that have grown out of the Suzhou tech bubble over the last six years. SJEC Corporation, the largest Chinese company producing elevators and escalators, was no match for many foreign competitors when it set up in the SIP in 2010. Today, the firm sells in over 100 countries and regions. Industrial parks have attracted technology, competition and collaboration with the best.

We meet Xu Ming, the Vice Mayor of Suzhou, inside a shiny block in the heart of the city. During the imperial days, Suzhou was a major supplier of food, she says. At the time, a large number of Chinese scholars routinely hosted by emperors during the feudal days were from this city. Today, most of the engineers accredited to the elite Chinese Academy of Sciences are from Suzhou.

Education and culture have been quiet drivers too. More than 30 foreign universities and colleges have established collaborative ties with Suzhou on innovation.

The ancient city's proximity to Shanghai (just an hour's drive) has brought with it good returns. The city has kept its natural environment, with green spaces, even in the face of rapid growth.

Suzhou has some fascinating ideas. On one side of the city lies an ancient town that covers 14 square-kilometres while on the western side a modern high-tech industrial suburb has sprang up.

We head to the Humble Administrator's Garden, one of the famous attractions in the ancient side of Suzhou, located in the northeastern corner of the city. It is the largest classical garden set up during the Ming Dynasty (about 500 years ago). Its existence is traced back to the reign of Emperor Zhengde (1506-1521) when the site was occupied by Dahong Temple. Legend has it that an imperial envoy and poet named Wang Xianchen started tending the garden around the site.

Its characteristics come across as being symbolic of many elements of life: calm in a deeply troubled mind.

The Humble Administrator's Garden consists of three parts; there is the East Garden, replete with ancient-style buildings, verdant lawns, ponds and a grove of crape myrtle trees. The West Garden has pavilions, small mountains and is largely dominated by water. The Central Garden is more of a theme park, with features that attempt to recreate the scenery of the fairy islands of the East Sea.

Kunshan City

Kunshan is a small county-level city under Suzhou, located 50km away from Shanghai and 37km away from Suzhou. The small city is one of the most economically successful county-level administrations in China and serves as a model city for ecological conservation, tourism and decent living.

Kunshan is the home of Kunqu Opera, one the oldest forms of Chinese opera and a performing art listed as a World Intangible Cultural Heritage by UNESCO. Away from the hum of the city, revelers sit inside Suzhou Kun Opera Theatre to watch performances of popular art.

Not far from the opera theatre lies Suzhou Embroidery Institute of China, a facility where a 4,000-year-old embroidery art is still being practiced today. Inside quiet rooms, groups of women sit behind looms, recreating beautiful patterns of paintings on silk cloth. Unlike brush and paper, the paintings here are produced using needle and thread. It takes about six months to finish stitching one art piece. One would think it's a time-wasting art until one finds out how much one complete painting costs. I come across one of the artworks displayed here, layered with glass and fine wooden carvings. It has a price-tag of $400,000!

Zhouzhuang Water Town

We then head southeast of Suzhou to Zhouzhuang, the oldest water town in China. Zhouzhuang is described as the 'Venice of the East' for the canals that give it enchanting watery views. The ancient town is more than 900 years old but retains the style and pattern of its ancient village. The existing structures, built during the Ming and Qing Dynasties, have been preserved as a tourist attraction.

We take a ride in a gondola, running through stone arch bridges and getting up-close with the city's past. Zhouzhuang was once a distribution center of food, silk, ceramics, arts and crafts in the south of China. Our gondolier breaks into an ancient song as she rows the flat-bottomed rowing boat using long oars as we glide on canals past ancient courtyards and imperial residencies spread across the tourist attraction.

Much of the city's economic gains can be traced to the Kunshan Economic and Technology Development Zone, set up in 1984 to boost foreign capital investment and export-oriented industries.

By the end of 2015, the KETD zone alone had attracted 2,170 investment projects worth $36.3 billion from 47 countries and regions, including Europe, America, Japan, Korea, Hong Kong, Macau and Taiwan.

By 2016, the entire city of Kunshan, with 2.5 million residents, had attracted over 7,700 firms from 56 countries with focus on electronics, biomedicine, robots and renewable energy.

A number of other industrial parks are also under development around Kunshan, focusing on robotics, finance, creative industries, advanced technology and food processing.

NANJING ►►

A suburb of Nanjing City, Jiangsu Province

Expansive road network

Tunnel road in Nanjing

SUZHOU ►►

A maze of expressways in Suzhou

Flowers sprout at the Humble Administrators Garden.

A charming Suzhou City

KUNSHAN ▶▶

Kunshan is a modern city

Gondolas are the best means of transport here

The writer at the Zhouzhuang Water Town in Kunshan City

Zhouzhuang Water Town attracts many tourists everyday

HUBEI

The city of Wuhan

Our journey across China takes us to the province of Hubei. It is not only one of the most prosperous provinces but also an important political and cultural hub of central China.

Hubei is an important cradle of Chinese civilization, with early traces of human existence here dating back to the Neolithic era. In recent times, Hubei has grown into one of China's most important industrial power bases.

In Wuhan, the provincial capital, ancient architectural designs, pagodas and cultural sites drive hordes of tourists to the area.

We drive on the Yangluo River Bridge, a suspended bridge built over the Yangtze River that spans 1,280 metres (4,200 ft), a feat of engineering and testament to China's mastery of construction technology.

Inside the heart of the sprawling city of Wuhan lies a tech hub known as Optics Valley, home to dozens of tech firms and start-ups. One of the firms that have built a strong base here is FibreHome, a home-grown tech giant and leading exporter of fiber-optic cables, data networking systems, wireless, and intelligent applications.

More home-grown and foreign tech firms are moving here in droves. Since the late 1970s when China's reform era started, the suburb has transitioned from a sleepy town into an important communications hub.

Public buses, taxis and subway lines are within reach. Green spaces are spread across the central business area to make room for decent living. It is a model of green development that has spread across the country.

Across city suburbs, local and western-inspired fashion brands, entertainment spots or fast-food chains sit side-by-side, screaming for the attention of passersby. Wuhan is a city on the move.

Like most thriving cities in China, the public transport system in Wuhan is quite organized. Wide roads, pedestrian and cycling lanes are well gazetted and marked. And green spaces are being preserved.

Transport hub

Wuhan lies along the middle reaches of the Yangtze River, the world's third longest river and important cradle of Chinese civilization. Taming the river for livelihood is a sacred duty in Wuhan as much as it is in the rest of China.

Wuhan's position as a major transport hub has attracted a large number of enterprises in the areas of infrastructure, energy and mineral resources, mechanized equipment, ICTs and agriculture.

With countless bridges and tunnels skirting across the city, Wuhan is ranked one of the most inter-connected cities of China. The city links Hubei to Central China and the rest of the mainland.

The city is home to the first north-to-south railway mainline to cross China. The railway line connecting Beijing to Wuhan was completed in 1905 and in recent years, it was extended to Shanghai.

The Yangtze and Hanshui rivers form the backbone of water, railway and road transport in this land, drawing such wealth to the entire Hubei province.

The focus on industry in this region went hand-in-hand with modernization of agriculture. Hubei remains an important agricultural region of China, traditionally known for cotton, rice, tea and wheat growing.

Cultural, economic centre

Wuhan is strategically located in the heart of central China and the Yangtze River Economic Belt, an important economic zone that accounts for 20% of China's GDP.

High-tech hubs and free trade zones have sprung up, focusing on major industries such as textile, petroleum and chemical processing, automobiles, machinery and power generation.

Numerous companies have set up shop in the high-tech zones, in clusters of high-end manufacturing in the fields of optical-electronics, telecommunications and laser technology.

Wuhan now hosts the annual Forum on Global Production Capacity and Business Cooperation, drawing thousands of business personalities and experts from across the world. Many are looking to learn from China's development story. Some are looking to tap into opportunities from China's push to invest overseas and establish international links.

By the end of 2015, at least 620 enterprises and institutions from Hubei province had overseas investments worth over $6b, spread across 70 countries and regions all over the world.

Therein lies an opportunity for those who want to do business with China. Hundreds of Chinese firms are going overseas, establishing connections and exploring opportunities.

Today, the region is one of China's top economic power bases, with GDP for 2015 exceeding $511b and a sustained growth rate above 10% annually. Income per capita in recent years has risen to $2,863.

History

Wuhan emerged as the political seat of the left-wing government of the Kuomintang after the 1911 uprising that ousted the Qing dynasty, giving birth to the Republic of China. The province holds many relics of the World War II battles. During much of the war, the eastern parts of Hubei were occupied by Japan while the western parts remained under Chinese forces. These influences are not hard to identify in the city's layout and major landmarks.

Culture, commerce and industry have thrived in Hubei since the ancient times. Early silk trade in Wuhan has been traced far back to the Warring States period (475–221 BC). So are the mining and metallurgy industries.

Culture, history, industry and technology are changing the face of Hubei. It's time for us to leave Wuhan and Hubei, in our quest for more of the China story.

WUHAN ▸▸

A busy suburb of Wuhan City

A production factory at FibreHome in Wuhan

A suspended bridge on the Yangtze River

A suspended bridge

A view of Wuhan City

Decent road network in Wuhan

Green Parks are spread across parts of Wuhan

WUHAN ▸▸

Wuhan has a well-developed transport infrastructure

Sprawling public transport network in Wuhan City

The city's sprawling road network

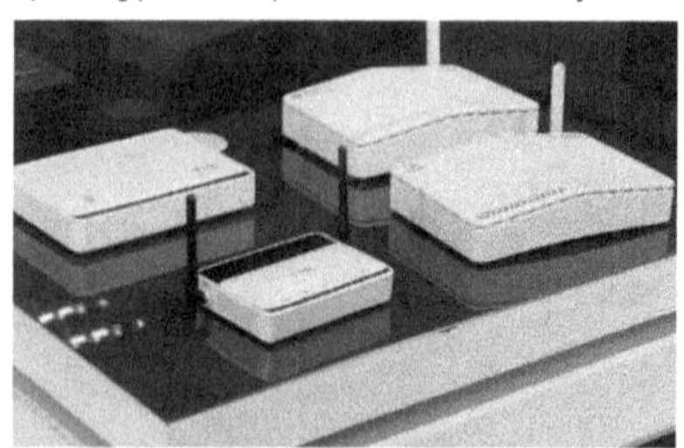

High-end communication devices at FibreHome

A view of Wuhan City

ZHEJIANG

Our travel across China leads us to the eastern coastal province of Zhejiang, one of the wealthiest regions of China.

Much of the terrain here consists of hills, plains, rivers and coastlines, around which a thriving tourism industry has been built. Archeological discoveries dating to the Neolithic Era and the Shang civilization have been made in this region. As far back as the Three Kingdoms Era (220–280 CE), Zhejiang was known as a region of tumult.

After the era of dynasties and kingdoms, a significant part of Zhejiang was occupied by Japanese forces. Rising from economic upheaval after the war in the mid 1940s, Zhejiang grew into a thriving industrial and agricultural base.

The province is well-connected by road, railways and ports, owing to the massive investment in infrastructure over the years. Known traditionally as the 'Land of Fish and Rice', Zhejiang is also a leading producer of cash crops such as cotton, and the largest producer of Chinese tea.

Zhejiang remains an important commercial and cultural centre, home to the famous Longjing Tea. China's ancient trade in wine, silk, paper, pencils, fans and dates is also traced to this region.

Hangzhou City

Drive around Hangzhou and you will know why Hangzhou is regarded in ancient honour as the 'Paradise on Earth,' along with Suzhou City. Hangzhou is not only the capital of Zhejiang Province, but also its largest city. It is also the province's economic, cultural, technological and educational center.

The city has a history dating back over 2,200 years to the Qin Dynasty, which introduced a county system of government. Today, the city is home to about nine million people. Hangzhou is renowned as one of China's 'Seven Ancient Capitals' and one in a cluster of designated historical and cultural cities.

An extensive network of highways, trains and coloured buses connect the city in more ways than one. In recent history, Hangzhou has emerged as one of the most economically vibrant cities of China, with numerous technology hubs – notably, it is home to global e-commerce giant Alibaba Group. Think of a city whose GDP for 2014 exceeded $135 billion, bigger than economies of many developing countries.

Hangzhou is one of China's smart cities with vast green spaces along major streets and suburbs, and a penchant for growth as a technology and innovation hub. We found the city brightly illuminated by night and sparkling clean by day, with rows of green along major streets and suburbs. In September 2016, Hangzhou hosted the G20 Summit, the first ever to be hosted by a developing country.

Hangzhou Cloud Town

Meanwhile, somewhere in the west of Hangzhou, we come across a village that is different. On a neat campus barely 3km from the city, a small tech village has been born: a place where youth meet to speak the language of software applications, e-commerce and cloud computing. The area features decent transportation, attractive green spaces and technology support infrastructure. Zhejiang plans to create 100 such villages across the province over the next three years as part of an upgrade of traditional industries, and a push to encourage innovation and promote tourism. Money is not the problem since about $81.5 billion has already been set aside for the project. Little wonder that Hangzhou is regarded as one of the happiest cities to live in and one of the most innovative cities of China.

We visit Hikvision, a company that grew out of this tech bubble to become the world's leading supplier of video surveillance products and solutions. From alarm systems to drones and smart bikes, the company set up in Hangzhou in 2001 is now a leading global brand. It is arguably more famous for its wide range of CCTV cameras. In 2015 alone, as many as 38 million cameras were produced by the company. In just 15 years, Hikvision has sold in 150 countries and acquired over 350 technology patents.

Tea Museum

Our bearings then lead us to the Meijiawu Tea Village, a famous tea plantation nestled in the hills surrounding West Lake. Once a poor village with a history of over six hundred years, local farmers started to plant tea and soon grew prosperous. This is the home of the famous Longjing (Dragon Well) tea. This part of Hangzhou is also famous for a rich tea culture that draws millions of tourists to the village every year. Tea culture in China stretches many centuries back in time and the beverage is a national treasure. There is even a national museum to showcase the history, types and characteristics of different kinds of tea culture. Tea in China can be offered as a sign or respect, reconciliation, reunion or gratitude. Meijiawu Tea Village is special not only for producing great tea, but also preserving an age-old tea culture.

West Lake

We take a boat ride across the West Lake, one of Hangzhou's most famous scenic spots. The still waters have inspired poets and painters throughout China's history.

Covering an area of about 2.5 square miles, West Lake is surrounded by other scenic attractions such as temples, pagodas, gardens, and artificial islands. The vastness of the lake, backed by the cool winds and surrounding natural vegetation, draws tourists to the area that has since ancient days been an important source of inspiration for travelers.

Some tourists opt to ride on canoes to get a different experience. One woman, seated alone in a canoe, scribbles something in a notebook as she rides on a boat guided by a rower. A white tinge forms above towering hills in the distance to create an enchanting pall.

Around the iconic lake, manmade features such as walkways, islands, bridges and gardens have been expanded to beautify a treasure that dates back more than 1000 years. In 2011, West Lake was declared a UNESCO World Heritage Site, sealing its place as a trove of history and heritage.

From a distance, the glittering skyline of Hangzhou City comes to the fore, blending easily with pristine views of mountains in a story of harmony between man and nature. Tourism has brought fortune to Hangzhou, a city of about eight million residents. Even with the rapid development, Hangzhou has kept its cool and left many parts of mother nature intact.

Jinhua City

There is a garden at Qiubin Primary School, somewhere in the quiet suburb of Jinhua, a prefecture-level city of Zhejiang province. The garden is not a repository of plant species but instead African cultural heritage. The garden, surrounded by the school's gleaming classrooms and administration blocks, has come to be known as the 'Dynamic African Park'.

At the park's entrance are two pillars shaped in form of a hut, a primitive dwelling still in existence in some parts of Africa. You will find sculptures of wild animals including an elephant, zebra, tiger and lion around the park. Besides, there is even a replica of the Pyramids of Giza. We get to tour the attractive park and one of the pupils explains in detail the characteristics of an African elephant, even though she has not yet seen one in real life.

The park is somewhat an almanac of African culture, music and fine art, where young Chinese students get up-close with the way of life of African people. Students are taught almost everything about Africa – from playing African musical instruments to creating handicrafts and some African attire. The African Park at Quibin was set up with the backing of Zhejiang Normal University, which itself was the first to introduce an entire institute devoted to the study of African culture. Prof. Liu Hongwu, an expert on African studies at the university, believes the park will promote China-Africa relations.

"A group of children who have fallen in love with African culture will be the bond of China-Africa non-governmental communication," Liu tells us during our visit to the school. The African garden is one of the experimental efforts to expose young Chinese students to the unique elements of African culture. Quibin Primary School has hosted students from schools in Africa.

The school with about 1,600 students embraces a multi-cultural environment. The students here have already embraced a more open view about Africans. One of them, Hu Lianwen, is eager to travel to Africa after learning about a few aspects of African culture.

"For some Africans, if their skin is a little white, they would be like us. If my skin is darker, I am also like an African," a school publication quotes one student as saying.

"African people are enthusiastic and civilized. We, Chinese people, are shy but Africans will say hello even to a stranger," another is quoted in the same publication.

In fact, Prof. Liu is confident such initiatives will raise a generation of Chinese children who have a "healthy, happy, open and inclusive spiritual world".

He believes that understanding African culture is important not just for improving communication but also out of shared history of civilization. "Africa is not only one of the cradles of civilization, but also a rising continent," he explains, noting that the two civilizations can learn from one another.

The efforts to improve language and communication is now two-way. Many universities and secondary schools in Africa, like in Uganda, are introducing Chinese language and culture classes.

Yiwu City

Our journey guides us south of Zhejiang to Yiwu, a county-level city that is home to the world's largest small commodities wholesale market. Yiwu is also one of the largest commodity export bases in China, with over 75,000 shops and stalls selling more than 1.8 million kinds of commodities. Most outsiders know Guangzhou as the most attractive trade hub in China but Yiwu might have much more to offer.

About 70% of the world's Christmas decorations come from this sprawling market covering a 5.5 million-square-metre business area. From artificial Christmas trees to toys, fashion clothing and jewelry, retail buyers from across China and the rest of the world flock here to negotiate deals on shipping containers. The attraction here is the relatively lower price and availability of almost anything. However, much of this trade is now migrating online as e-commerce giants like Alibaba tap into the lucrative market.

Yiwu enjoys unique advantage of proximity to megacities such as Shanghai (just 300km away). The city is inter-connected with a huge network of expressways, an airport and a busy port.

But the Yiwu Commodity Market represents much more than just trade: it symbolizes a culture of enterprise of the local community. In 1982, the market area was a laidback town where farmers met to sell small wares. But in a space of 30 years, makeshift stalls have been replaced by an International Trade Mart, a huge block divided into districts featuring tens of thousands of stores.

The growth and expansion of the market has in turn spurred development in an erstwhile rural town. Through the efforts of its citizens, Yiwu has grown into one of the most successful cities in

China. The market attracts more than 210,000 visitors daily. Goods from Yiwu Market are exported to 219 countries and regions. Each year more than 570,000 containers have to be exported from Yiwu. There are now over 3,000 permanent representative offices of foreign enterprises, and at least 13,000 resident businessmen.

One of the foreigners who have found fortune in Yiwu is 40-year-old Sourakata Tirera, a Senegalese businessman who opened a small company here ten years ago. His wealth was by 2016 estimated at over $300 million. Sourakata has gained celebrity status as one of the mediators whenever the traders have disputes, thanks to his fluency in Chinese, French and English.

Such a huge population of traders certainly comes with all sorts of dispute and the mediation team is one approach supported by the city government to maintain harmony.

HANGZHOU ▸▸

Hangzhou City

Tea plantation at Meijiawu Tea Village in Hangzhou

Hangzhou by night

YIWU ▸▸

A suburb of Yiwu

African art collection in Yiwu

PICTORIAL

YIWU ▸▸

Yiwu Trade Centre

QUIBIN SCHOOL ▸▸

Africa-themed artwaorks produced by pupils

Chinese pupils play African drums

Pyramids of Giza Jinhua Qiubin Primary School

Jinhua Qiubin Primary School teaches pupils about Africa

SHANDONG

The city of Qufu

A giant statue of the ancient philosopher Confucius peers down at moving vehicles on a sprawling network of neat roads as you leave the main airport in the city of Qufu, in Shandong province.

The buildings here retain elements of China's ancient past, yet the plush cars on the neat roads tell a whole different story. The streets speak of a harmonious blend between the ancient and the modern.

For many centuries, Shandong emerged as a land of immortals, philosophers and a vibrant economy. Besides Confucius, Shandong is the birthplace of influential thinkers as Sun Tzu, Mencius and Mo Tse.

Our first attraction in Qufu is the Confucius Temple, a gated compound built and maintained by successive Chinese emperors in honour of sage, Confucius. Inside the expansive compound, the philosopher's way of life is meticulously recreated and relived.

Here is a serene enclosure full of trees, most of which are still intact after hundreds of years.

Confucius lived between 551BC - 479BC. He is revered as the 'greatest sage and teacher' in China but the influence of his teachings has been spreading across the world over the many centuries.

He is inspiration for the belief system known as Confucianism. At the Confucius Temple, the philosopher has been deified and some of the people who visit the temple burn incense in worship of him.

Numerous gates lead to different parts of the deeply revered temple. And these gates, for some reason, symbolize something deeper in Chinese tradition. Outside the temple, residents cash in on the ancient philosopher's legacy by selling artworks inspired by his fame and teachings. Herein lies a story about the strength of cultural tourism, and with it, the gift of domestic tourism, as more Chinese people travel back into time to discover more about their heritage by visiting the attractions at home.

Just a few yards away sits another attraction built in memory of him, known as the Confucius Mansion. It was built for his descendants and called the Masion of Lord Yang Sheng. It comprises 560 halls and rooms used as government offices who held numerous positions in the imperial government for several generations.

Confucius' effigies stand out in parts of downtown Qufu. Even centuries after his death, he is still so revered that he has an overbearing presence in this town.

His gravesite is one of the most sought-after attractions. The Konglin Cemetery is a vast site set aside as burial grounds for Confucius and his descendants. There are multiple gates, passageways and rows of trees that lead to the actual place believed to hold the remains of Confucius.

The Confucius Compound, consisting of a temple, mansion and cemetery, was listed by UNESCO in 1994 as a World Cultural Heritage site.

The legend of Confucius has inspired tourism in numerous self-effacing suburbs of Qufu. It is a story that keeps telling; a parable retold and spread across the world. Our journey into Qufu must end here.

Jinan City

An hour's bus ride from Qufu leads us to Jinan, the capital city of Shandong province. We arrive in this bustling city as darkness sets in, but the lights are already bright against a pall of darkness. The night comes to life as buildings light up in a rainbow of colours. People gather into well-manicured public squares, just to have fun. Youth perform karaoke or just walk around well-designed public spaces. Many people here are living the Chinese dream.

In the morning we visit Inspur, a home-grown firm that is now one of the largest IT companies in China. From humble beginnings in the 1960s, the firm has grown into one of the biggest software and engineering suppliers. In 2015 alone, its business lines raked in $10b, and with it 3,500 patents. Globally, the firm has built itself a name across 104 countries in the world of cloud computing, processors, servers and supercomputers. After generations of breakthroughs in technology, the firm now runs an e-government cloud for several cities and e-commerce platforms, and provides data processing for satellites and big data for taxation, banking and transport.

In the second quarter of 2016, Inspur ranked second globally in a high-end market for Unix, an operating system, just behind IBM. Such is the scale of ambition for Chinese companies.

We take a journey back into history when we visit the Shandong Museum which holds a trove of information about the people of Shandong and the history of Chinese civilization. For one reason, some of the early discoveries about human existence were made in this province, in an area known as the Shandong Peninsula, along the lower reaches of the Yellow River, South of the Bohai Sea and to the west of the Yellow Sea. The central and eastern parts were covered by forests, which were favorable for hunting and gathering. The northern and western plains were good for agriculture while the southern parts had a mix of forest and grassland, making the areas desirable for human settlement. This geographical disposition pertains to this day.

Some of the early technologies relating to stone tools, jade making, textile, wine brewing, sculpting, medicine, writing, divination and the calendar unearthed in Shandong are exhibited inside the spacious museum that holds thousands of ancient artifacts. Some of the items are said to be dating back 10,000 years.

By day, Jinan is a city on the move. Upscale shopping malls at every turn, imposing architectural designs and an extensive road network reflect the changing face of the fast-growing city.

We visit the China National Heavy Duty Truck Group or Sinotruck, a state-owned truck manufacturer, the largest in China with roots in Jinan. Rolling off assembly lines in the 120,000-square-metre workshop are cylinder blocks and vehicle parts for a chain of heavy trucks produced by the firm.

Founded in 1956, the firm produced China's first heavy truck three years later and now boasts of a growing market in over 90 countries. It turns out that after years of hard work, research and integration of German technology, the Chinese have now built independent technologies including advanced engines that rival the best in the world. The determination to excel, the ability to take risks and patience to harness ideas from other people are takeaways.

It's time to leave Jinan and head to one more city in this land of surprises.

Qingdao City

We travel by high-speed train to the city of Tsingtao, also pronounced 'Qingdao,' a fast-paced coastal city dotted with numerous capes and bays.

We start off at the National Agricultural High-tech Zone in Jimo. From aquatic gardens to green houses, it serves as a demonstration area for farmers on advanced farming practices to improve yields. Little wonder this part of Shandong produces much of its own food, a story replicated across many of China's provinces and regions. Investment in research and modern farming has guaranteed that China feeds her people with less reliance on food imports.

We drive through a network of neat roads in the verdant plains of Tsingtao and come to a halt at the home of Haier, a famous brand in the field of home appliances. From manufacturing refrigerators to washing machines, cameras and a range of kitchen appliances, the company has grown into a household brand.

But beyond the fine displays of high-end appliances showcased at the company's museum lies a story of a revolutionary corporate culture in China that is traced back to the firm. In 1984, a young general manager named Zhang Ruimin was posted to the firm, then still known as the Qingdao Refrigerator Plant. The company was just starting to break into the home appliances market but was making losses and was on the brink of failure. Employee morale was low. Ruimin gathered that his early tasks would be to confront not only the financial ruin but also a disastrous employee work ethic.

Some of the notices issued by Ruimin to employees banning insolent acts are still on display inside the company museum. Yet, he did come to learn that the endless list of regulations alone would do little to stifle the deplorable work ethic.

In 1985, when confronted by a customer about the quality of a fridge, he promptly ordered an inspection of all new fridges and discovered 76 faulty new fridges. In those days, many firms paid little attention to quality. His next move is what shocked many, even beyond the borders of China.

One breezy morning, Ruimin gathered the workers in a yard outside the plant and with the help of a sledge hammer, he ordered that all the gleaming fridges be smashed to pieces, one by one.

"If we don't destroy the 76 defective refrigerators, we will make 760 defective refrigerators tomorrow and 7,600 the day after tomorrow," he is quoted in a video many years after the incident.

"Outwardly, we smashed defective products but inwardly, what we smashed were defective ideas in the minds of our staff," stated Ruimin about his uncompromising attitude towards quality.

The sledge hammer he used to correct a defective culture hangs inside the company museum, alongside a collection of photos, notes and relics that tell the company's journey.

In Qingdao City, across China and overseas, Ruimin's unflinching stance on quality is credited for inspiring a novel culture of respect for brand building.

Within one year, the change of employee culture and introduction of new technology had earned the company profit of one million yuan (about 520 million Ugandan shillings), up from a loss of almost 1.5 million yuan the previous year.

Haier's story is now a case study in global business schools and over the years grew into a management philosophy that embodies some form of radicalism in pursuit of innovation and excellence.

What started in 1955 as an electric appliances repair cooperative is now a global multibillion electronics firm commanding 9.8% of the world's home appliances market. Needless to mention is that this is a state corporation. And so that's what appears to be the fighting spirit of Qingdao, where numerous brands have sprung up and a host of foreign firms have set foot. Elements of western technology and Chinese business values have blended here in many ways than one. And Chinese brands are evolving alongside some of the more established names in different business fields the world.

In the heart of Qingdao, high-tech zones in such fields as marine engineering, machinery, energy and biomedicine continue to attract many of the big brands. This sprawling city has come of age. Travel around the city and you find decent transport infrastructure – from electric buses to an expansive road network with green outlays.

Qingdao City is credited as the capital of Chinese brands, home to several renowned brands such as Haier, Hisense, and Tsingtao Beer. Each of the brands carries with it stories that have shaped its journey of growth over the years, synonymous with China's rise.

Qingdao had become one of China's model cities along the Eurasian economic corridor and continental bridge under the One Belt One Road. The city is now home to high-tech zones covering such fields as marine engineering, machinery equipment, home appliances, energy and biomedicine.

In 2015, Qingdao's GDP exceeded 930 billion yuan ($137b), marking an 8.1% growth from the previous year, with maritime revenue accounting for 22% of the fortunes.

Our trip in the city of Qingdao leads us to the home of Tsingtao Beer, one of the most popular brands in China. Beyond being an alcoholic drink, the beer brand in many ways represents an important part in Chinese history and culture. In 1903, it was established as the first beer factory in China by British and German businessmen.

The two-storey factory building still exists today. Its expansive floor area, granite wall base and red brick wall with a roof incline are features that have all been kept intact for more than a century. In 1897 German troops occupied Qingdao. Later in 1916, the Japanese took control of Qingdao and managed the beer brand for almost 30 years. In 1945, the Kuomintang government repossessed the brewery and rebranded it. In 1993, while still experimenting with reform of state enterprises, the brewery started operating as a private company and was listed on the stock market in Hong Kong and Shanghai.

Today, it is rated the sixth largest beer company in the world and sells in more than 80 countries. With the rise of beer culture arose surprising trends in the consumption culture. In the 1970s the people of Qingdao drank beer in canned jars. In the 1980s they drank the beer from large bowls and in the 1990s they packed it in plastic bags. Today, the beer is sold in well-designed beer bottles and cans.

While the Chinese suffered occupation, they harnessed the technologies and refined them to improve their lives. Some of the equipment dating back more than a century is still kept intact. At first, the taste of the beer was determined by the people who controlled the process. Today, the beer brand is produced according to Chinese tastes. And, guess what: there's more to beer than just the beverage at this factory. Ever heard of barley tea? At the souvenir shop, we come across nuts, tea and trinkets inspired by the beer culture.

In the evenings, people come together to sip on beer. Little wonder Qingdao has been described by different titles, including being the 'most livable city' and the 'happiest city'.

Qingdao's early interaction with the West is evident in landmark buildings and architectural designs strewn across every street.

We drive on the famous Jiaozhou Bay, the world's longest sea bridge spanning over 26km that connects the thriving northern part of Qingdao with the island and the industrial suburb of Huangdao. Beneath the bridge is the Jiaozhou Bay tunnel, a 6km under-sea road linking Huangdao to the South of Qingdao. And such is the marvel of engineering and experience that the Chinese people are proud to show the world. Infrastructure and connectivity have brought this port city this far.

In Huangdao district we tour Qingdao Port, a century-old port that has grown to be the world's seventh-largest in terms of cargo volumes. It maintains shipping routes with 700 ports across 80 countries and regions. In recent years, the port has expanded connections with countries in Asia, Europe and Africa.

In this part of Qingdao, we come across one of the home-grown enterprises, Hengshun Zhongsheng Group, a multi-billion firm dealing in such areas as high-tech power grid equipment, clean energy, industrial parks and finance, with interest in expanding business overseas.

It's time to leave Shandong province, a bustling city of like contrasts – a province where tourism, agriculture, industry and transport are driving China's economy.

QUFU

A street in Qufu city

A stone tablet on a mound of soil believed to be Confucius' resting place

The writer with friends at the Confucius Temple

JINAN

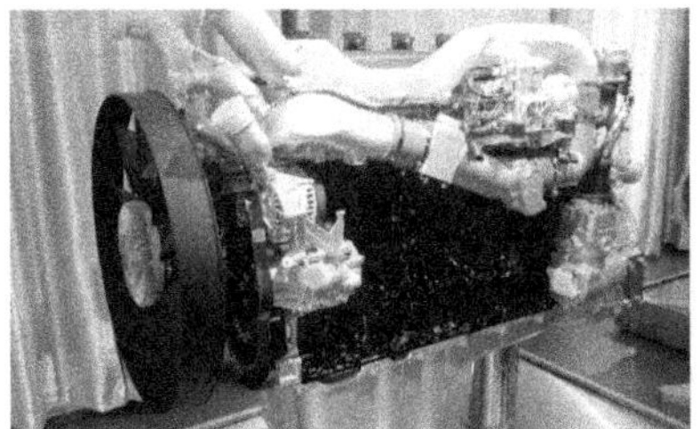

A design for an engine produced by Sinotruck

A street in Jinan

JINAN 

A Street in Jinan City, Shandong Province

TSINGTAO

A cargo ship destined for Liberia, Africa

A power transformer produced by Henshung in Qingdao

Qingdao Beer Museum

Beautiful city

GUANGDONG

Here we are, in Guangdong, the most economically prosperous province of China in terms of GDP volumes. Guangdong is situated in the southern part of China, adjacent to Hong Kong and Macau. The Pearl River, the third longest in China, runs through the province. What this means is that the region is a fertile ground for agriculture but there's much more to it. With humid sub-tropical and tropical climates, the average temperature here is around 22°C. Little wonder that Guangdong is now China's most populous province, home to about 106 million people. Over 30 million Chinese nationals overseas hail from this region.

Guangdong witnessed many historical events in China's recent history, including the Opium War and the 1911 Revolution that ousted the Qing Dynasty and created the Republic of China. Guangdong province was one of the pioneering bases for China's era of reform and opening up initiated by Deng Xiaoping to attract foreign capital, investment and new ideas for development.

Over the last 30 years, Guangdong has achieved remarkable economic and social development. In 2015, its GDP reached $1.2 trillion, emerging as China's wealthiest economy. If Guangdong were an independent nation , it would rank as the 16th largest economy in the world or 9th in terms of export and import volumes.

Guangzhou City

What we find in Guangzhou, the capital of Guangdong province, turns out to be exactly what it is described for: industry, trade and connections with the outside world.

Known as the 'South Gate' of China, Guangzhou is located north of the Pearl River Delta, adjacent to Hong Kong and Macau. The city's proximity to the two special administrative regions has placed Guangzhou at the centre of global trade, all backed by its strategic location at the heart of the Pearl River, the third longest in China. Guangzhou enjoys a long history of over 2,200 years as the cradle of the Ancient Maritime Silk Road, a trade hub that cut through Asia, Europe, the Middle East and parts of Africa.

In 2015, the GDP of Guangzhou City reached $291.3b (roughly 12 times the size of Uganda's economy). Its most distinct feature is the Canton Fair, held twice a year since 1957 and still attracts exhibitors from over 50 countries. During the Cultural Revolution, most of the ports along China's coastline were closed but Guangzhou remained open. There are probably more consulates in Guangzhou than any other city in China. After years of embracing the reform and opening up era, Guangzhou, home to over 16 million, is now a major economic power base and transportation link across southern China.

We tour the suburb of Dengfeng that has come to be known as 'Little Africa.' Thousands of Africans have either settled here or regularly flock to this place in pursuit of business opportunities. I never saw such a large community of Africans anywhere in China than I did in Guangzhou. Some simply believe the native Chinese people from this region are more open to foreigners.

One-third of all trade between China and Africa is in Guangdong, a province that is now host to the Investing in Africa Forum, which links Chinese enterprises to investment opportunities in Africa.

With about 400,000 Africans living there, Guangzhou hosts the largest African community in Asia, who are living off a thriving import-export trade. And it is here that I meet Hamza, a Ugandan trader based in Guangzhou. He says the city has opened doors for him and several other traders who regularly import merchandise for retail business in Kampala.

"The prices for items here are relatively cheaper since there are numerous wholesale markets situated next to factories," he explains. From shoes, kids' and women's clothing or electronics, 'Little Africa' is a scene of bustling trade, with hundreds of retail and wholesale shops spread across entire streets.

About 40% of all Africans in China live in Guangzhou, according to Luo Jun, the deputy director general of the foreign affairs office of Guangzhou. "They are helping to strengthen trade and ties between China and African countries," he says.

"Chinese people here are friendly and easily accept foreigners and new ideas. These are the features that have made Guangdong prosperous," explains Jun.

Authorities in Guangzhou set up a reception centre in Dengfeng to help foreign nationals settle into Guangzhou through an elaborate process of orientation. Volunteers at the centre offer free Chinese language classes to visitors and help with lodging registration, policy consultation, health maintenance, social assistance and cultural exchanges.

On the outskirts of central Guangzhou, we visit the Guangzhou University of Chinese Medicine, where researchers are confident they have come up with the most efficient malaria drug.

Marketed as 'Artequick,' the tablets contain Artemisinin and Piperaquine as active ingredients. Studies in the Comoros and Nigeria have shown outstanding results in the fight against malaria, researchers say. But the drug would still require approval from the World Health Organization, which recommends Coartem, a combination of artimether and lumefantrine for malaria. Nonetheless, Chinese drug manufacturers are emerging as major players in health. 90% of all drugs used to treat patients in China are locally produced.

We then head southward to the district of Nansha, which offers some clues on Guangzhou's rapid rise over the past two decades. Part of this journey started in 1997 with the creation of Nansha Information Technology Park, gradually transforming a sleepy area into an industrial complex. Then, there was a shift towards more advanced industries. Nansha district would be elevated into a free trade zone thriving on the heart of the Pearl River Delta. Today, the area has morphed further into an international shipping and logistics hub stretching as far as Hong Kong and Macau.

From there, our next stop in this bustling city of Guangzhou is the famous Canton Tower, the highest tower in China and third-highest in the world.

Nothing epitomizes the rapid development in Guangzhou than the speed at which an elevator lifts you from the ground to the top floor of the 600-meter-high tower! At that height, the world is at your feet and nothing can describe the feeling of peering down at insect-size skyscrapers and the mighty Pearl River. And there are records the building that opened in 2010 has already broken: world's highest horizontal Ferris wheel bubble tram, highest outdoor observation deck, highest heart-pumping vertical free fall sky drop and world's highest revolving restaurant.

Guangzhou has certainly come a long way and the landmarks of this journey are evident. And like most urban cities, taming the rate and scale of urban growth will be a challenge. The city is undergoing some form of transformation. It will be a different city in the next ten years.

Shenzhen City

We drive on a very long expressway to Shenzhen, a city situated at the east estuary of the Pearl River. In this city lies one of the most successful stories of China's reform and opening up era, when Shenzhen became the first special economic zone. Opening up the market for foreign investment and private enterprise was a risky gamble that soon paid off in just a few years as dozens of foreign brands settled in the area. By 2015, the GDP of Shenzhen, a city of about 11 million residents, had a GDP of $281b, equal to that of Ireland, and larger than Finland's ($223b) and Portugal's ($199b).

There is, perhaps, no better place that narrates the history of the city than the Shenzhen Museum, an imposing 32,000-square-metre building in the heart of Shenzhen. Videos, photos and artworks capture Shenzhen's reform process inside this grand building with gleaming walls. But the process comes across as having been far less rosy, especially at the beginning. The ribbon-cutting ceremony was by way of a blast on a mountain to pave way for Shekou Industrial Zone. The Chinese army had to deploy 20,000 construction engineers who were joined by thousands of labourers from across China. The living conditions for the workers soon became hard but they kept going. Within five years, the fruits of the ambitious work were visible as skyscrapers sprouted all over. That is how Shenzhen earned its name as 'the city that rose overnight' or 'instant city'.

In 1990, the Shenzhen Stock Exchange, the first of two in mainland China, was established. By 2016, the Shenzhen Stock Exchange was ranked 7th in the world in terms of market capitalization. Today, the gleaming skyline of Shenzhen is an illustration of a story of hard work, ambition and dedication.

We get to visit several home-grown companies to understand why Shenzhen is such a force. One of these is Tencent, the world's fourth-largest internet company by revenue. Founded in 1998, the company has a wide reach in media, entertainment, payment systems, internet, mobile phone value-added services and online advertising services in China. Perhaps, the company is better known for the revolutionary instant messaging app WeChat that had over 900 million users by the end of 2016, along with several other digital platforms.

We also visit the home of Huawei, one of the world's largest tech firms, launched in 1987 with capital of about $3,000 and now valued at over $140b.

Huawei is the world's third-top-selling smartphone brand after Apple and Samsung. Almost every electronic gadget today has components made by Huawei. Beyond the buoy of growing revenue, the companies in Shenzhen are turning tables on global corporate culture. Take

Huawei for instance, whose founder and helmsman, Ren Zhengfei owns less than 1.4% stake in the firm, leaving the rest to its 85,000 employees. Then there is the management system where the firm's day-to-day operations are run by three executives, each holding the position of chief executive on rotational basis every six months. The idea behind it is simple, according to Zhenfei, who introduced the leadership style after observing the intricate migration of birds in a 'v' formation.

Our tour of Shenzhen leads us to the headquarters of Mindray, one of the world's largest manufacturer of medical devices ranging from imaging, patient monitoring, life support and in-vitro diagnostics. Growing out of an early reform bubble in Shenzhen in 1991, the company's products have found their way into healthcare facilities in over 190 countries across North and South America, Europe, Asia, Africa and Australia.

We also visit the home of DJI, the Chinese firm that commands about 70% share of the world's commercial drone market, much in part due to the popularity of the Phantom series. Drones, known technically as Unmanned Aerial Vehicles (UAVs), were traditionally developed for military and surveillance purposes. DJI saw a niche and soon dominated the market for commercial drones used for recreation, film, photography or even agriculture.

The profile of companies that have sprouted out of Shenzhen is almost distinct. Unlike in most cities like Shanghai, the companies that were born in Shenzhen were largely private enterprises.

China's economy is currently undergoing major changes that will see the east Asian nation significantly reduce reliance on manufacturing and exports to drive growth in the coming years. Shenzhen is one of China's most dynamic and globally-competitive economies. It started with very little and the companies here have risen to the top through hustle and innovation. It is envisaged that within a few years Shenzhen will surpass Shanghai.

A new cluster of industries is emerging in Shenzhen, with focus more on life sciences, virtual reality, artificial intelligence, robotics, space technology and wearable technology. Imagine what this city will look like in the next 20 years. It's no surprise Shenzhen is dubbed the world's tech capital. In 2015, Shenzhen had more applications for patents than France and UK.

Zhuhai City

Every two years, the city of Zhuhai in China's southern province of Guangdong has something to show to the world. Inside large exhibition halls the latest aviation technology in display, from advanced fighter jets to civilian aircraft, flight systems, engines, radars and drones. It is what is known as China International Aviation and Aerospace Exhibition or Zhuhai Air Show. The 2016 edition might have had much more to reveal.

Crowds of aviation enthusiasts fill a barricaded ground to watch daring acrobatic maneuvers by pilots in flying horses. The deafening roar of the fast-flying jets and dazzling aerial stunts keeps thousands of spectators facing upward to the skies. Since 1996, the air show has been held in Zhuhai, showcasing advances in Chinese technology to the world. Foreign exhibitors also display their wares. Observers in military circles watch keenly as China's advanced fighter jet, the J-20 fifth-generation stealth fighter and the Y-20 military transport, take to the skies, highlighting a leap in Chinese technology. On the sidelines of the airshow countries take part in trade forums to discuss cooperation in aviation.

GUANGZHOU ▸▸

An aerial view of Guangzhou from the top floor of the Canton Tower, the third tallest in the world

Guangzhou has an elaborate transport system

A street in Guangzhou

SHENZHEN ▸▸

A gavel used to transfer of land tenure system in Shenzhen

A statue of Deng Xiaoping laying ground for Shenzhen Special Economic Zone.

SHENZHEN ▸▸

A suburb of Shenzhen

ZHUHAI ▸▸

A formation of jets at the 2016 Zhuhai Airshow

Zhuhai city

The airshow provides a platform for aviation cooperation

The writer with friends at the 2016 Zhuhai Airshow

SICHUAN

Our journey across China leads us to the southwest. Sichuan, one of the largest provinces in China, is surrounded by vast plains, hills, mountains and plateaus. It plays an important role in China's history as one of the places where early discoveries about human existence are traced. The region is said to have been highly developed during the ancient Shu civilization about 25,000 years ago. The fertile agricultural region is famous for its cuisine characterized by spicy and pungent flavors.

Home to about 1,700 (85%) of the world's giant panda population, Sichuan is also home to rare plant species, beautiful landscapes and distinct culture, including the famous Sichuan Opera. The province, one of the most populous with 91 million residents, is also one of the most connected in terms of transport, with over 6,100km of expressways and 4,000km of railway.

Sichuan was one of the first provinces to undergo limited experimentation with market economic enterprise in the late 1970 under Deng Xiaoping (1978 – 1989). One out of two iPads held by anyone anywhere on the planet was produced in Sichuan. Today, Sichuan's towering beautiful landscapes and historical relics have made the province a major center for tourism. Its GDP for 2015 exceeded $460 billion, equivalent to China's national GDP at the start of the reform and opening up in 1978.

Chengdu City

Chengdu, the capital city of Sichuan, is the cultural and industrial center and one of the first centers of printing in the country. The first widely used paper money in the world was issued here. The city saw a lot of fighting during the 1911 uprising that overthrew the Qing Dynasty and served as an important base for allied forces during World War II. After the war, Chengdu grew into a large industrial base for manufacturing, aluminum smelting, chemicals and fabric. The city is now one of the pilot areas for an ambitious development model that places more emphasis on smart living.

Today, Chengdu is one of the most important economic, financial, commercial, cultural, transportation, and communication centers in western China. The city will become only the third after Beijing and Shanghai to have two airports, owing to an increase in passenger flights.

The sheer scale of the city's economic power is evident in the sprawling apartments, global brands and transport network. Originally a production base for textile and electronics, Chengdu has evolved into one of China's core base for modern hi-tech industries in automobile, aerospace and military fields. Since 2,000, the city has hosted the Western China International Fair, an annual gathering of business and technology firms from over 76 countries.

A few miles away from the city's central business district, we visit the Chengdu Hi-tech Zone where clusters of global tech firms have set up. If the profile of foreign companies that operate here is anything to go by, Chengdu is truly an attraction – companies such as Pratt & Whitney (aircraft engines), Texas instruments (semiconductors), molex (fibre optics) are here. The zone, since its establishment in 1988, has attracted many domestic and foreign investments, including over 300 of the Fortune Global 500 businesses. With clusters of industries in electronic information, biomedicine and precision machinery, it is one the leading national advanced hi-tech development zones of China.

Our first stop in Chengdu is in the small town in Wenchuan County, where an 8.0 magnitude earthquake left at least 87,000 people dead or missing almost 10 years ago.

At exactly 2:28:01pm on May 12, 2008, a sudden force shook the earth with such devastating force that left the people of Yingxiu town little room to make sense of the natural terror. Huge boulders hurtled down the mountain slopes, cars were trapped along a busy highway and chaos stirred the quiet neighbourhood, displacing more than 4.8 million people.

A walk through the memorial hall located at the hillside of Yuziki village brings to light the devastation, captured through real-time footage of the catastrophe, photos and simulated film. Aircraft wreckage on display and images on a giant screen inside the museum retell the horror of a rescue helicopter that crashed in the mountains as crew tried to find trapped survivors.

A policeman rushing to help was crushed inside a small van, and the mangled wreck of a van in which he was travelling lies still inside the museum. In a dimly-lit room, an elevated platform recreates the terror through sound and light effects panic. Suddenly, the platform jolts and sways to give tourists a terrifying feel of the incident.

The Wenchuan earthquake is regarded as the most destructive and humanitarian relief challenge since the founding of the People's Republic of China. A high school dormitory crumbled with the weight of the earthquake.

Several strong aftershocks, landslides, mud-rock flows, quake lakes and inclement weather further complicated rescue and relief efforts. At least ten other provinces, including neighbouring Gansu and Shaanxi, suffered damage resulting from the earthquake while tremors were felt as far as Beijing and Shanghai.

Official records indicate that the vicious quake created 104 dangerous barrier lakes, damaged 1996 reservoirs and created more than 6,000 geological disaster spots.

A major highway that connected several communities along the mountainous region was brought down, cutting off communication. The cost of the destruction in Wenchuan was estimated at $135b, which included rebuilding destroyed homes and major transport lines around the affected areas.

But out of the tragedy arose a spirit that brought people from across China and overseas to join hands and help deliver relief items to people trapped by the earthquake. Images of long lines of volunteers holding hands and lining up from the lowlands to the peak of the mountains to deliver relief items are testament to the enduring spirit of sacrifice.

The Sichuan earthquake also inadvertently cast the spotlight on areas that seemed to have been left behind by development. Consequently, this led to an ambitious drive to rebuild the area, and the efforts are paying off.

The main highway skirting around the mountains has been rebuilt. Down below the hillsides is Shuimo Town, an eco-village where a community of minorities enjoys decent living standards.

Shuimo is located 76km from Chengdu and sits on the edge of the Shouxi River, an estuary of the Minjiang River, dating back to the Shang Dynasty. The ancient-style buildings have been preserved.

Although none of its residents was killed, about 30% of the homes were affected by the earthquake. The disaster inadvertently drew attention to their low living standards.

Rows of neat homes surrounded by green have given new face to the natives. Each of the families has a decent home, access to water and electricity and spacious gardens. The affected areas been reconstructed as have a decent township model. A new seismic-resistant hospital was built with funding from a charity sale by three painters and designed by renowned engineer He Jingtang. It is regarded the most advanced quake-proof hospital in China, able to withstand a magnitude 9.0 earthquake. In fact, doctors performing an operation would be unfazed by a magnitude 7.0 or lower earthquake.

At least 200 similar eco-villages have been built around Wenchuan under a poverty alleviation plan. About 3.8 million people in Sichuan still live below the poverty line. The provincial government targets to have everyone here moderately prosperous by 2020. The reconstruction efforts around Wenchuan County after the 2008 earthquake serve as a model for rural development. The area's unique features have become a thriving attraction for tourists in Sichuan from across China and all over the world.

Dunjiangyan

We then head west of Chengdu City to see the world's oldest irrigation system that still tames floods and supplies water for farming in Sichuan. The Dujiangyan irrigation system was built over 2,300 years ago (around 250 BC) under the guidance of Li Bing, at the time governor of the Shu Prefecture of the Qin State. It started with an innate desire to control incessant flooding on the Minjiang River that wreaked havoc across the vast Chengdu Plain.

Part of the astounding engineering project involved cutting a channel through the surrounding Mount Yulei. In the middle of the river a dyke was then created, dividing it into two: an inner river and an outer river, each with its own distinct function.

Two spill ways were built at the end of the dyke, creating a gravity irrigation system that soon stopped the floods, yet at the same time diverted water for agriculture.

Since its construction two thousand years ago, agricultural production has improved and the size of irrigated land expanded, from 126,000 hectares to over 660,000 hectares covering 36 counties.

The ancient irrigation system made Sichuan the most agricultural production region of China and still draws thousands of tourists and scientists from across the world for leisure or study.

It is testament to the genius of early Chinese scientists in a land that was, until a generation or two ago, lagging in terms of modern technology. During World War II, planes that sought to bomb the dam and cripple Sichuan and parts of southern China could not find the dam because of its unassuming design.

The Dujiangyan consists of three parts: Yuzui, a 'fish-mouth' dyke; Feishayan, a spillway for discharging flood and silt, and the Baopingkou, a channel cut through Mount Yulei.

During the flood season, the Yuzui dyke diverts 40% of the water from the Minjiang River into the inner river while 60% of it is pushed into the outer river, helping keep a balance.

However, during the dry season, the reverse is what happens. The system also pushes 90% of silt into the outer river, ensuring that the main Minjiang River is free from debris that leads to floods.

The Baopingkou, shaped like an inverted ladder, plays the function of regulating water flow while the Feishayan spillway discharges flood and silt from the inner river into the outer river.

Dujiangyan is both a scenic spot surrounded by mountains and a UNESCO World Heritage Site. In his honour, a shrine was built in remembrance of Li Bing on the east side of Dujiangyan.

There is a suspension bridge connecting the artificial island to both banks of the Minjiang River. Made of wooden plates and bamboo handrails, walking across the bridge is a thrill as it sways with every movement. It is known as one of the Five Ancient Bridges of China.

Up-close with the giant panda

Our travel through Sichuan takes us to the Dujiangyan Panda Conservation and Research Base, the home of the giant panda. We find the cute bears regaling in an afternoon nap, unstirred by the prying eyes of dozens of very eager tourists. Teasingly, one by one, they come out of their lairs to munch on bamboo. Their distinctive black patches on white around the eyes, over the ears, and across rotund bodies make them spiritedly attractive. Coy and evidently proud, the giant panda is a national treasure in China, and many people are endeared to it much more for its calm demeanor.

Sichuan is home to about 80% of the world's panda population. They largely feed on bamboo, but not just any type. At the facility, research and breeding is done to guarantee that the rare species will be in existence for many more years to come. Hundreds of tourists visit the conservation area to catch more than just a glimpse of the adorable bear.

Tianfu New Area

Somewhere on the outskirts of Chengdu, China is building a model city in what is known as the Tianfu New Area. Simply put, here is an area covering 1,578 square-kilometres where a small city will sprout, full of science and technology development zones. To achieve this plan, at least three cities, seven counties and 37 townships will be merged to create a single hub. The project was officially launched in December 2011 with the aim of reconstructing a modern international urban area combining industry, modern housing, high-end manufacturing and services. The area will be linked to the city's new airport, high-speed railways and expressways and other regional transport hubs and traffic facilities in Chengdu, up and ready for operation by 2020. Such is the model of development being rolled out across China that integrates environment, business, modern living and innovation.

Next, it's time for a trip back into time with a visit to the Temple of Marquis Wu, situated on the southern outskirts of Chengdu City. The temple was first built in the 6th century in memory of Zhuge Liang

(181-234), a chancellor of the state of Shu during the Three Kingdoms period (220-280). Due to his great wisdom, he was considered the greatest military strategist of his time.

Also part of the Temple of Marquis Wu is the famous Jinli Street, a 550-metre-long walkway replete with buildings of the Qing Dynasty style. There are many bars, inns, snack stores and souvenir shops and attracts an estimated 18 million tourists every year.

We visit the Jinsha Site Museum which displays the archaeological finds said to be dating back more than 3,000 years and highlighting the civilization of ancient Shu Stat. In the ancient times Sichuan Province was called Shu State. Gold articles, stone statues, trinkets and farming tools dating back to the ancient times have been uncovered at the Jinsha Site.

One attribute of the Chinese people is that they have kept their history intact even in the face of modernization.

CHENGDU ▸▸

An suburb of Chengdu City, Sichuan Province

DUJIANGYAN ▸▸

A recreation park in Djiangyan

The writer with friends at the Dujiangyan

PANDA ▸▸

One of the giant pandas

Tourists at the Panda conservation facility in Dujiangyan

SHUIMO ▸▸

Children at a community shelter in Wenchuan

Souvenir market in Wenchuan

JINSHA SITE MUSEUM ▸▸

Golden mask at the Jinsha Site Museum

Stone tools at the Jinsha Site Museum in Chengdu

WUHOU SHRINE ▸▸

Jinli Street in Chengdu

Statue of Zhuge Liang at the Wuhou Shrine in Chengdu. He is considered the greatest military strategist in China

You never leave Sichuan without tasting hot pot

Wuhou Shrine

TIBET

The last 20 minutes of our four-hour flight from Beijing to Tibet are no less than a lull: a silent pause, as we glide just above tall mountains. Tibet is located in the southwest of Qinghai-Tibet plateau, on the south of Xinjiang province, west of Sichuan province, southwest of Qinghai province and on the northwest side of Yunnan province.

On arrival at the main airport in Tibet's capital Lhasa, our hosts welcome us warmly and each of us is presented with a Khata – a type of silk scarf – as a symbol of blessings.

Lhasa City

A bus ride from the airport to the heart of Lhasa takes us through a vast stretch of plains, nestled between snowy mountains that appear to touch the sky. The enchanting beauty of Tibet comes to light in the heart of Lhasa, a landscape that perfectly embodies the religious and cultural traditions of the Tibetan people.

Towering over major landmarks in the city is the iconic Potala Palace. Built in 1645 and now a UNESCO World Heritage Site, the palace is considered by Buddhists as one of the holiest places on earth.

The magnificent 13-storey palace is built right into a mountainside and comprises over 1,000 rooms that once acted as the home of the Dalai Lama, and the political and religious centre of Tibetan Buddhism.

Contrary to the picture of Tibet conjured in the minds of many, Lhasa is a modern city peppered with giant shopping malls and facilities that speak of one region's journey and development.

Tibet is one of the five self-governing autonomous regions of China, occupying one eighth of the country's territory. With an altitude averaging above 4,000 metres, Tibet is often called the 'Roof of the World' or 'Third Pole of the Earth.' It is home to the world's highest peak, Mt Everest, and the source of the Yangtze and Yellow rivers, both bedrocks of Chinese civilization.

But this high altitude means extremely low levels of oxygen and harm to one's health if caution is not exercised. At such high elevation, air is thinner and every step you make appears to suck out the little oxygen already in your lungs, leading to headaches, fatigue, exhaustion and in extreme cases, asphyxiation (death). Prior to the trip, we had been given a long list of things that we could not do in Tibet; like taking a shower on the first day, performing strenuous activity, walking fast or eating too much.

During our five-day tour, everything we had been warned about somehow came to pass. I suffered from high altitude sickness and was at some point hooked onto an oxygen tank. However, make no mistake, these circumstances have not caused tourists to shun Tibet.

Tibet is a dream destination, drawing more than 20 million visitors every year. It is home to 3.2 million people, most of them ethnic Tibetans with a long history dating back about 4,000 years. Most Tibetans speak their native Tibetan language and Mandarin.

A large number of them live a pastoral lifestyle and earn a living farming and tending yaks (cows). Most of the local inhabitants practice Tibetan Buddhism and visit pilgrimage sites including the Potala Palace and Jokhang Monastery, which are the most famous Buddhist temples. Hundreds of pilgrims walk clockwise around temples with prayer wheels in hand, in a Buddhist custom believed to bring about longevity, good health and fend off bad luck. Apart from 46,000 Buddhism adherents, about 6,000 Muslims and over 500 Catholics practise their faith freely, officials say.

The Jokhang Temple located in Barkhor Square is considered the most sacred temple in Tibet. It was founded during the reign of King Songtsen Gampo around 652BC. According to tradition, the temple was built for the king's two brides: Princess Wencheng of the Chinese Tang dynasty and Princess Bhrikuti of Nepal. The two brides are said to have brought important Buddhist statues and images from China and Nepal to Tibet. The temple is now a UNESCO World Heritage Site as an extension of the Potala Palace.

We set out in the evening for a spectacular performance that is all about Princess Wencheng. Some historians claim Wencheng opened Tibet to trade with China along the ancient Silk Road and carried dowry for her marriage to the king that included gold, furniture, silk, porcelain, books, jewelry and musical instruments. She is also considered to have introduced modern methods of agriculture with her grains and farming tools, as well as skills in weaving, construction and writing.

Standing tall in the heart of Lhasa is the Potala Palace, formerly the chief residence of the spiritual leader, the Dalai Lama until the current (14th Dalai Lama) fled to India in 1959. Besides its 1,000 rooms, the magnificent palace comprises 10,000 shrines and about 200,000 statues.

Before the 1950s, Tibet was under the rule of a theocracy – headed by the Dalai Lamas. It became a part of China following a 1951 agreement in Beijing. But the current Dalai Lama (Tengyin Gyatso) fled into self-imposed exile after falling out with the mainland China government after the agreement. He still insists on Tibet's autonomy from China.

In 1965, Tibet became an autonomous, self-governing region albeit with oversight from the central government.

With some form of Marshall plan, government has heavily invested in infrastructure and social welfare programmes for the Tibetan people. Still, Tibet is regarded as one of the poorest regions of China.

There are 590,000 people classified as living below the poverty line but the province hopes to get them out by the year 2020. At the same time, Tibet is one of the fastest-growing regions of China, having recorded double-digit growth figures for the last 20 years. In 2015, Tibet's GDP exceeded 100 billion yuan with 11% growth, higher than the national average of 6.9%.

Majority of the natives (about 2.3 million farmers and herdsmen) have been relocated to modern housing facilities where they have access to postal, telephone and internet services. Life expectancy has improved from 35.5% in the 1970s to 68% today, and at least 80% of residents have access to broadband services. Education, health and living standards have also improved significantly. By 2020, Tibet will be poverty-free and every household will be moderately prosperous, says Jiang Jie, the vice governor of the autonomous government of Tibet.

By the way, Lhasa is a city as spiritual as it is modern. Expanding mazes of huge expressways and urban construction projects have put the city on a new path: a delicate road to finding a new balance. We make a stopover at the Tibet New Energy Research and Demonstration Center, founded in 1981, where experiments in solar energy, wind energy and biogas are driving transformation. For one, solar parks spread across the province generate 14 megawatts, more than half of Tibet's 23 megawatts output.

We then move on to the outskirts of Lhasa City to a school where we find students clad in camouflage uniform and helmets erecting a brick wall within minutes. The teenagers execute their work with the kind of speed and dexterity that defies their youthful looks. They are students of Lhasa No.2 Middle Vocational and Technical School, one of the top vocational schools in the province. Tibet does not enjoy the economic status of China's major provinces like Guangdong and Jiangsu. But education is one of the bridges to development. The students here are entitled to 15 years of free compulsory education, compared to nine years for children in more developed cities. In one class at this school, a group of students is busy at work, connecting circuits and assembling electrical parts in an engineering class, all under the guidance of an instructor.

Then, there is another group of performers showcasing traditional Tibetan culture through music while another group is seen carving images and designs into blocks of wood to produce artworks. One other group carves steel plates and folds bands of iron used for construction. China has taken leaps in science, engineering and technology and has built a strong base of skilled workers by focusing on skills development in the country's education system.

Today, Tibet has a huge network of railway lines, highways, tunnels, bridges and airports linking the geographically challenged region to other parts of China. Many of the workers recruited to work on the projects are natives. On the outskirts of Lhasa, construction of a 5,476km highway (the longest in China) connecting Tibet to Sichuan, Shanghai and Nepal is under construction, cutting through mountains.

Nyingchi

We travel southeast of Tibet to the prefecture-level city of Nyingchi, which means 'Throne of the Sun' in Tibetan dialect. Here lies one of the most ancient cities in Tibet that is home to more than 10 minority groups.

Nyingchi is also known as 'Linzhi.' The city is described as a 'Natural Museum of Nature' or 'Switzerland of Tibet' because of its breathtaking natural scenery that includes huge snow-capped mountains and alpine gorges. Nyingchi is one of the important cradles of ancient Tibetan civilization, with early records tracing human settlement to the region as early as four or five thousand years ago. Linzhi is home to China's largest primitive forest with over 2,000 rare plant species including tall trees, medicinal herbs, fungus and rare wildlife species such as Tibetan lions and musk deer.

Cultural tourism is big business in Nyingchi. In Lulang Town, there are not enough upscale lodging facilities for foreign tourists. So, the natives offer their homes to visitors as part of a cultural experience and charge a modest fee for accommodation and meals.

Travelling to Tibet brings you up-close with the rare beauty of an ancient culture, unique wondrous terrain, holy sites and a different face of China. It's time to leave Tibet in pursuit of another miracle.

LHASA ▶▶

Iconic Potala Palace, the home of Tibetan Bhuddism

Lhasa is a spiritual capital as much as it is a modern city

A street in Lhasa

Live performance about Princess Wencheng

The writer with friends at a public square in Lhasa

This Tibetan family offers its home for tourism

A more upscale hotel with Tibetan features

Snow-capped mountains of Nyingchi

The writer with a group of friends in Lulang

Horse riding is a popular attraction in Lulang

SHANGHAI

We arrive in Shanghai on a chilly afternoon but the charm of this large metropolis cannot be hidden. Shanghai is the largest and most prosperous city in mainland China. It is also the economic, finance and cultural center of China.

Shanghai is a modern and fast-paced city, rich in history and culture and often referred to as the "Paris of the Orient" or "Pearl of China". It is one of the four direct-controlled municipalities of China, with a population of over 24 million residents.

Yet that's not all. Bordering the provinces of Jiangsu and Zhejiang to the north, Shanghai is also a major transport hub with the world's busiest container port. The province is located along the Yangtze River Delta and sits on the southern edge of the Yangtze River at the heart of the Chinese coast.

Shanghai's prominence as a major administrative, transport and commercial hub has its origins in China's turbulent past, including the Opium War and colonial treaties that placed it under British occupation. In many ways, the province epitomes foreign rule that saw it at one time under not only Britain, but also France, US and Japan – each having their take either through concessions or outright occupation. The city rose to become a financial hub across the Asia-Pacific region and by the 1930s was teeming with factories, printing press and maritime trade.

In the late 1970s, with the expansion of finance and foreign investment reforms introduced by Deng Xiaoping, Shanghai underwent rapid development and transformation. Cloud-piercing skyscrapers, museums and historic buildings dot every corner of the city. Today, Shanghai is one of China's most industrialized and cosmopolitan cities, vastly interconnected through a large network of expressways, two airports and a high-speed railway.

If you are not enchanted enough by what you see during daytime, you needn't worry, for nothing beats the sight of Shanghai at night. Unrivaled views of its past and future occur on a boat cruise on the Huangpu River in the heart of the city. An amazing sight and great spectacle it is when major buildings light up the night sky! On the western shores lie a string of colonial landmarks, reminders of the city's 19th-century struggles. Yet on the eastern shore, the steel-and-glass skyscrapers showcase the Pudong New Area that has flourished into a financial empire of the future. As the boat turns around, stunning views unfold of the space-hugging skyscrapers that keep changing colour. Talk of the Shanghai Tower or the Bund.

At a dizzying 632 metres, the Shanghai Tower is the world's second-tallest building. Its curved façade and spiraling form have been likened to the dynamic emergence of modern China. In some way, it symbolizes Shanghai's rapid transformation since the early 1980s when the area was still a sparse collection of warehouses, factories and low-rise residential buildings. Within a space of 30 years, the city has turned into a dense pool of glittering skyscrapers that appear to be competing for attention.

An elevator gets us to the top floor of the Shanghai Tower in no time – what with a gravity-defying top speed of 20.5 metres per second! A slight buzz in your ears is inevitable by the time you get there, but once at the top, the view beneath is incomparable.

The night life in Shanghai is vibrant. In the evenings people take walks across city streets or hang out in public squares. Youth perform karaoke, fly kites or just sit in the open spaces to live the moment. Dozens of coffee shops, restaurants and entertainment spots are spread all over the sprawling city. Shanghai is where it all seems to have begun.

Pudong Miracle

But, it turns out the bright lights of Shanghai have come at a high price. Decades of painstaking efforts helped turn the sleepy suburb into a thriving metropolis. It all started in Pudong. We meet one of the people who took part in these early efforts, Mr. Zhao Qizheng, who heads the state council information office. Qizheng, a leading scholar in public diplomacy and international communication, was a young engineer in the 1970s. He recounts how initial success of Shenzhen prompted Shanghai to be considered as a pilot reform area. At first, the eastern part of Shanghai was the least developed compared to the western part that was already an industrial hub. So, the early attempts to develop Shanghai focused on addressing the development imbalance. Shanghai then set out to be China's window to the global economy, with links to London (UK) and Frankfurt (Germany) in Europe.

"We invited foreign consultants to help us plan the urban area but Chinese experts had the final say on the blueprint," Qizheng narrates about the initial designs for Pudong.

A hi-tech hub was soon set up to attract foreign and local industries. In 1980, there was one railway line and one airport in Shanghai. Today, Shanghai has two airports but they are not enough; the third one is under construction. In the 1990s, economists predicted that the Pudong reform model would be a failed test. At the beginning, it was such a herculean task, Qizheng says, as the city set out to attract investment from the more prosperous provinces of Jiangsu and Zhejiang. Ten hectares were demolished to create a green zone and a lot of money was spent to relocate people from the area. Pudong Airport was built along with the highway. Laws and regulations were too rigid to attract foreign investment.

Some foreign companies that set up wanted to produce for the local market but they were encouraged to produce for export in exchange for tax rebates. They managed to convince German carmaker Volkswagen (VW) to enter into a partnership with them to produce sedans – passenger cars – but the venture was initially unsuccessful and the production line shut down.

Then entered US carmaker General Motors (GM). When the automaker's market tumbled a few years later and all production lines were not making profit, it was the Shanghai plant that saved the entire corporation, recalls Qizheng. The wages of Chinese workers employed by the corporation were one seventh that of US workers who went to work in Shanghai. Within a short time, the number of sedans sold in China exceeded that of cars sold in the US market. And so, Shanghai transformed from a centre for textile trade into a thriving manufacturing hub with factories sprouting all over Pudong.

As the city developed, its story had to be replicated in other provinces of China, which required technology transfer. However, by the 1990s, the technology that changed Shanghai was obsolete, so authorities rejected calls to transfer antiquated equipment to other municipalities. So today, Pudong has a new skyline. Most of the old factories have been either shut down or moved further to the countryside. Shanghai still attracts foreign investment but in new kinds of industries.

Economic and market reforms were not a smooth ride, even in Shanghai, which is one of the cities with the earliest interaction with the Western world. Qizheng recalls how one investor asked him whether there was a hospital within a 20-mile radius. Another one asked if there were thieves in the neighbourhood. When the old man convinced the investor that the area was peaceful, the investor still wondered whether bringing money to the area would not breed thieves.

"Winning the trust of foreign investors, not skyscrapers, was our driving force for investment in Pudong," says Qizheng.

Shanghai had to send delegations overseas and hosted foreign experts to assess the local environment regarding rental pricing, transport, user fees and security. Today, Shanghai produces as much as one third of China's trade with the rest of the world. The city is home to the world's fifth-largest stock market by market capitalization at $3.5 trillion by February 2016.

For developing countries to get out of the snare of backwardness, they must adapt innovative financing models. To achieve this, Qizheng proposes two ideas: one, build infrastructure and use it as collateral for international funding. Secondly, introduce operate and transfer agreements with foreign companies, allowing firms to build infrastructure, operate it for a few years and hand it over to government. Qizheng is now a dean at the school of journalism, Renmin University of China.

We visit the China Executive Leadership Academy in Pudong, a cadre school for Communist Party. Established in late 2005, the institution is considered one of the top four party schools in China. It's a decent block surrounded by a neat, well-manicured compound. Leaders from China's provinces meet in rooms for special training sessions on leadership, a preserve for top government officials and civil servants. They are even trained to handle crisis moments – anywhere from uprisings to epidemics and natural disasters.

"Crises and opportunities occur within a very short time. Every leader should be innovative, coordinate responses and maintain calm during a crisis," explains Prof. Li Yijing, an instructor at the facility.

Prof. Zhou Zhongfei, the academy's executive Vice President, says such sessions are more about preparing competent leaders. Civil servants are reminded about the country's political system of 'socialism with Chinese characteristics' and its ideals.

On the outskirts of Pudong we meet Prof. Feng Weizhong at Waigaoxiao No 3 power station, the world's cleanest coal power plant. Nine years ago, Feng designed a system to improve efficiency and reduce emissions from the coal plant that supplies about one-third of Shanghai's energy needs. After many years of research, Feng's work is helping China to generate electricity and remove harmful sulphur compounds from coal. China is slowly phasing out outdated coal power plants in favour of cleaner sources such as solar, wind and nuclear. Much of this pursuit relies on advanced boilers and turbines used in clean coal power.

Weizhong's technology has allowed the plant to operate far below the national and global average emission standards for emissions from coal power stations. Plumes of white smoke billow out of chimneys at Waigaoxiao coal plant but he explains that this is steam. His next step will be to design a system to transform the steam into water for use at the plant. Feng's genius has made him famous but he remains humble. We meet him a few weeks before he is scheduled to address a conference in the US about his ground-breaking '5E' Technology.

Feng has been called the 'Thomas Edison of China' for the technology that has been rolled out to at least seven other coal-fired power stations in China.

Shanghai Pilot Free Trade Zone

Next up, we visit the Shanghai Pilot Free Trade Zone, the first free trade zone in Mainland China established in April 2013 under the country's new economy development strategy. The area initially covered 28.78sqkm consisting of four bonded parks. It was expanded to cover a larger area of 120.72sqkm on April 27, 2015. By the end of March 2016, up to 34,000 enterprises had set up in the SHFTZ, ranging from trade, services, finance, transport, culture, education, healthcare, construction and real estate.

So what was so important about the SHFTZ? First, authorities developed and published the first 'negative list', which is an outline of the sectors in which foreign investment is prohibited or restricted, among them national security, public order, public culture, financing regulation and government purchases. For all sectors that are not on this list, foreign investors are accorded equal treatment as domestic companies in China's free trade zones. Over the years, the 'negative list' has been shortened and administrative procedures shortened to ease investment access in free trade zones. China currently has 11 free trade zones spread across different provinces. Apart from Shanghai, there are free trade zones in Chongqing, Henan, Hubei, Liaoning, Shaanxi, Sichuan, Zhejiang, Fujian, Guangdong and Tianjin – the last three as recent as 2015.

City Temple of Shanghai

We take a walk around the City Temple of Shanghai, a folk temple located in the old city of Shanghai. It was built in honour of three Chinese figures elevated to 'city god' status in line with ancient tradition. Features of the temple have been kept intact since around 1403 during the Yongle era of the Ming dynasty. The popular temple is always teeming with tourists. In the past, residents of the old city as well as nearby areas visited the temple to pray for good fortune and peace. Today, the temple has attracted many businesses being set up in the area, turning the surrounding streets into a busy marketplace.

On the outskirts of central Shanghai, we visit *The Paper* (Pengpai News), a media firm that has taken a very radical approach to journalism. Using mobile-based aggregator tools, *The Paper* has a daily reach of over 10 million people, turning out to be one of the most influential sources of news in mainland China. Taking advantage of a large online presence through platforms such as WeChat and Weibo, *The Paper* provides the fastest and in-depth coverage of politics, society, economy, opinions and culture. It is owned by Shanghai United Media Group, an arm of the Shanghai Municipal Party Committee. Although with links to the ruling party, *The Paper*, which went online in 2014, does not shy away from controversial topics such as corruption scandals. It offers some insight into the future of mass media in a fast-changing marketplace.

Museum of Mergers and Acquisitions

Question: How did Shanghai grow into one of the world's leading financial centres? One place that offers insight into this journey is a building in Putuo District, on the outskirts of central Shanghai. It is the world's first museum devoted to mergers and acquisitions. Visitors learn about important elements and history of the global financial market through a wide range of films, photos and exhibits.

Important quotes from some of the world's most influential thinkers and business leaders hang on walls in different sections of the iconic building. Visitors get to know about the evolution of the financial industry in Shanghai and the rest of China. Museum of Mergers and Acquisitions is the fifth museum in China dedicated to the finance industry. Similar museums have been set up in Tianjin, Suzhou, and two in Beijing. Tracing the history of money is important to China, which is slated to take its place as the world's largest economy. The seals, ink-stones, paper currency and gavels collected over the years and put on display inside the museum will be potent reminders about caution, risk and ingenuity in global finance.

Our last stop in Shanghai turns out to be the home of the Commercial Aircraft Corporation of China Ltd, a state-owned aerospace firm preparing to challenge Boeing and Airbus in the passenger aircraft market. We get up-close with the first domestically-built passenger aircraft – the ARJ-21, a short-medium range turbofan regional aircraft and the C919, a large civil jet aircraft. The aircraft reflect a fighting spirit that has defined the past, present and future of Shanghai. The spirit of enterprise, innovation and entrepreneurship.

Shanghai night sky

An upscale mall in Shanghai

Prof. Feng Weizhong, the engineer behind the world's cleanest coal plant- Waigaoxiao No 3 power station

A suburb of Shanghai

Network of express ways in Shanghai

Zhao Qizheng, one of the people who shaped the rise of Shanghai in the early 1980s

Model of C919 passenger aircraft

A column of towers in Shanghai

Shanghai City Temple

Glittering sky in Shanghai

NINGXIA

The last few minutes of our flight to Ningxia Hui Autonomous Region in northwest China offer a clear view of the harsh, rocky terrain below, surrounded by a rambling desert landscape. The scenery slowly starts to change upon descent to the main airport in the capital, Yinchuan, where patches of green vegetation sit in the middle of the unforgiving terrain.

Yinchuan City, the provincial capital, is a modern city surrounded by rows of finely pruned trees and shrubs stand out on either side of the roads and on the islands. A large network of expressways connects the city to far-flung districts where development projects are transforming the rugged landscape.

The province is home to about 6.8 million residents and is dominated by Hui ethnic minorities, who constitute more than half of the population. Ningxia is a landlocked region, far from the nearest sea port. Out of this difficult terrain are over 60 historical sites including mosques, pagodas, pavilions, temples, and imperial tombs that are important tourist attractions.

Ningxia, which means 'Peaceful Western Xia,' has its origins in the Western Xia Dynasty. The province is located in the ancient 'Silk Road,' placing it at the heart of an important trade route connecting China to Europe, Asia and parts of Africa. The Yellow River, an important cradle of Chinese civilization, remains a lifeline for the province.

Yinchuan City

Yinchuan's central business area is filled with architectural designs and symbols inspired by Islamic and Arab culture. You would be forgiven to think you stumbled into one of the thriving cities in the Middle East. Not surprising that most of the people who live here are Muslims. Cozy public gardens spread across much of the fast-growing city's outlook, with verdant trees and artistic symbols of Arab and Islamic tradition.

There is an imposing structure in the heart of Yinchuan's central business area known as the Ningxia International Hall, home to an e-government public cloud. All residents here are registered onto a central database at the facility. Officials say it makes it easy to keep track of population demographics or interact with citizens. Doctors attending to patients at health facilities in Ningxia can consult their colleagues in Beijing via video conferencing. Real-time updates on weather, housing or traffic are relayed from this hall. Yinchuan is a smart city.

Ningxia used to be the poorest region in China. In 1982, a team from the United Nations visited the area and their report was no less than a scathing indictment. "They described it as one of the places on earth that are not fit for human beings to live in," one official from the provincial administration recalls. The poverty rate was as high as

74.8% and the living conditions were terrible. Many people lived in the hillsides and nothing seemed to grow out of the dry landscape.

To improve the living standards, authorities have had to relocate communities from condemned buildings on the hillsides to decent community apartments in the low lands. About 1.2 million people were relocated and their lives have been transformed. 98% of the people in this region have medical insurance and senior citizens have a special shelter.

Students from ethnic minority communities now have access to free education, breakfast and lunch at elementary schools and middle schools. The training here is tilted towards vocational education. Ningxia is one of the labour-exporting regions sending out over 600,000 people to work in other provinces, and as a result remitting home about $1 billion every year.

Tapping into the Yellow River, an extensive irrigation system had to be set up to extend water to remote areas in the central and southern parts of the province that grappled with water shortage for many years. For the more far-flung areas the local government has pumped billions of money into large-scale water projects and constructed over 200 reservoirs to extend water into the dry lands. Today, most communities in Ningxia have access to safe drinking water.

A vast network of canals and irrigation projects has increased acreage of farmland in Ningxia to over 100,000 hectares by the year 2016. Ningxia is today the largest producer of wolfberries in China, and farmers here export fruits, flowers and vegetables to other provinces in China and overseas.

The revolutionary steps it took to transform Ningxia have helped to bring down the rate of poverty incidence from 25.6% in 2011 to 14.5%

in 2015. Although the region's economy pales in comparison with those in more developed provinces, its rapid rise from a GDP of $188 million in the 1980s to $35.2 billion by 2016, represents a significant leap. Farmers' income per capita has increased 46-fold, from 126.6 yuan ($18.5) to 6500 yuan ($955). More than half of the residents now live in urban areas and at least 434,000 people have been lifted out of poverty in the last five years. But the task is not yet over. By 2016, at least 581,000 people in this region were still living below the poverty line. The regional government has set itself a target to ensure every resident is out of poverty by the end of 2018.

Ningxia is a geographically challenged region. With a desert area that covers about 1.6 million hectares, the development efforts here involve taming the desert. Farming and herding practices three decades ago created the desert. In 1998, government took a stand to protect the ecological environment and subsequently banned farming and herding along the hill slopes. A programme was initiated to convert the area into forest in order to let nature heal itself. Hundreds of farmers earn a living by planting shrubs in square boxes and trees across the vast dry lands. By 2016, over 86,000 hectares of forests stood on erstwhile desert land. As a result, sand storms and soil erosion that ravaged the region are slowly being controlled. It is in this area that China first piloted the straw checkerboard method, a revolutionary technique of planting a type of weeds in desert land. Slowly, vast tracts of dry lands are being transformed into pristine forest landscapes.

The economy of Ningxia has had a turn-around in recent years as a result of massive efforts to turn a dry landscape into a commercial hub linking the province to the Middle East and Africa, where religion and culture are unifying attributes. New highways have been completed, connecting a previously desolate suburb to a growing industrial town.

About 43km southeast of Yinchuan lies an area that was once more of a wasteland but has today emerged as a modern industrial town. Home to over 38 billion tonnes of coal, the rugged landscape is now home to the massive newly-built Ningdong Energy and Chemical Base. But what do you do with such huge reserves of coal at a time the world is getting rid of the 'dirty fuel?' In recent years, major reforms have come up to switch from coal to cleaner energy sources like wind and solar. Construction of new coal fired plants has been halted. China is the largest producer and consumer of coal in the world and much of the country's domestic electricity is still derived from coal.

So, at the Ningdong Energy and Chemical Base, in the heart of a sprawling dry land, coal is not only being used to generate power but also to harvest natural gas, liquid-fuels, plastics, building materials. Nothing seems to go to waste.

The local communities here live in harmony, irrespective of their ethnic or religious differences. Hui Muslim minorities account for 36% of Ningxia's population, alongside other religions that include Buddhism and Catholicism. Although Islam is the dominant faith, social harmony is preached extensively. Every year in September, a day is set aside to promote harmony and peaceful coexistence.

YINCHUAN ▸▸

Developed area in Yinchuan

RURAL DEVELOPMENT ▸▸

A kindergarten for the less privileged

A shelter for the elderly

Apartments for the less privileged

The writer with students at Yucai Senior High School

DESERT CONTROL AT BAIJITAN FOREST RESERVE ▸▸

Straw checkerboard technique used to turn arid parts of Ningxia Province into a green paradise

NINGDONG ENERGY AND CHEMICAL BASE ▸▸

A growing suburb on the outskirts of Ningxia

New roads in the arid parts of Ningxia

Ningdong Energy Base

Ningdong Energy and Chemical Base

LIAONING

I take a high-speed train from Beijing to Liaoning Province, located in the northeastern parts of China. The name 'Liaoning' has different meanings but the common one is 'distant peace,' derived from the province's ancient and early modern experience with turbulent times.

In ancient history, Liaoning was part of the Korean Kingdoms, later the Ming Empire in 1371, Manchuria before it fell later to the Qing Empire in 1644.

In the 20th century, during the Russo-Japanese War between 1904 and 1905, many key battles took place in Liaoning. Once the dust of war was settled, Liaoning emerged as one of the first provinces in China to industrialize, initially under Japanese occupation.

In the 1950s and 1960s, Liaoning became home to one of the largest iron and steel industrial bases in China, with multiple heavy industries springing up there.

Covering a total area of 145,900 square-kilometres, the terrain of Liaoning oscillates between highlands in the west, plains in the middle, and hills in the east.

With an estimated population of 44 million inhabitants, Liaoning is today one of the largest provincial economies of northeast China.

In 2015, its GDP exceeded 3 trillion yuan ($500 billion) with per capita GDP of about $7,400, making it one of the seven largest economies of China.

Liaoning contains some of the foremost paleontological sites in the world, with fossil discoveries made in the region during the early 1920s.

The province remains one of China's most important industrial bases, with clusters of industries in minerals, machinery, electronics, petroleum and construction.

Shenyang

Shenyang is not only the provincial capital of Liaoning, but also the largest city in northeast China by urban population, with at least seven million inhabitants.

Its ancient and early modern history as the capital of the Qing dynasty and colony of the Manchu people (17th century) comes to light in cultural relics and architectural designs around the city.

The expressways that skirt around the city lend credence to the city's status as a major transport hub linking China's northeast to the country's neighbours Japan, Russia and Korea.

Like most cities across China, Shenyang is home to clusters of hi-tech, economic development, free trade and export-processing zones built to catalyze development in north-eastern China.

Under a new era of modernization, the city has created vast planned areas to attract domestic and foreign firms in advanced industries such as bio-medicine, clean energy and communication.

PICTORIAL

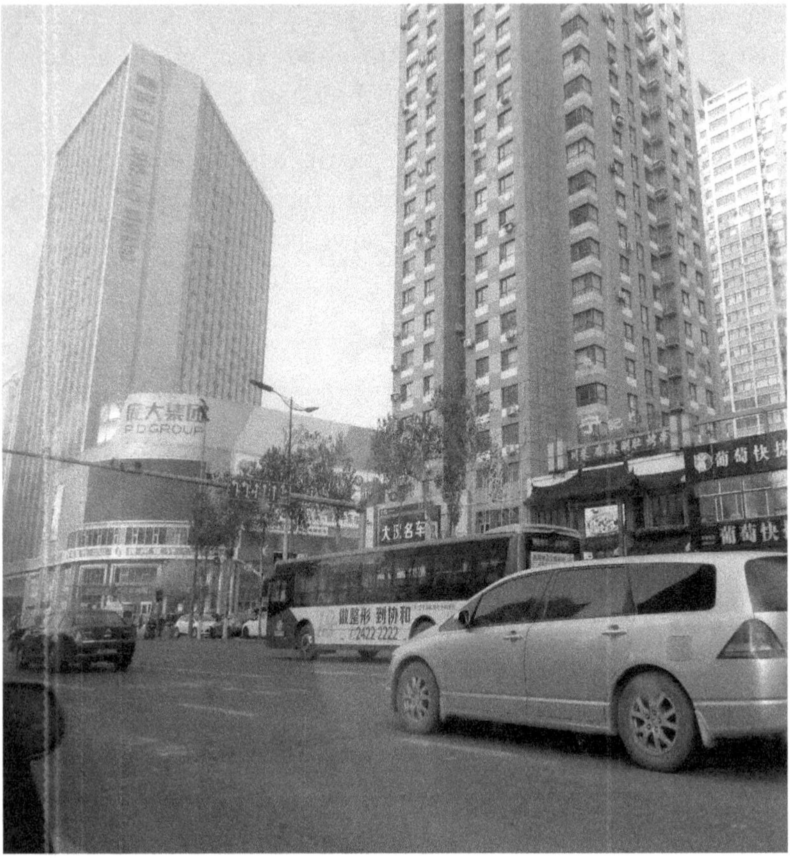

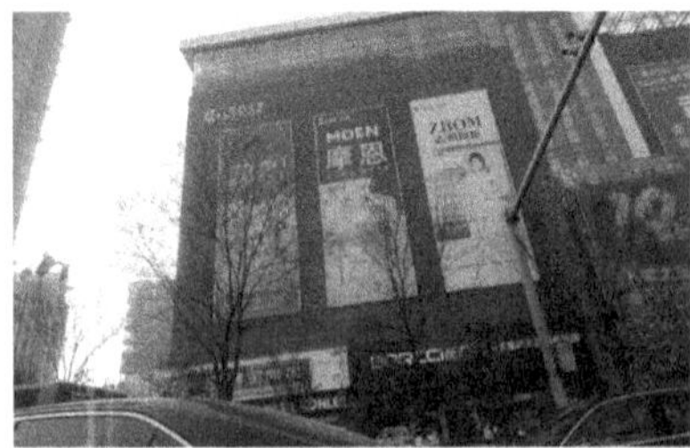

A street in Shenyang

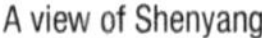

A view of Shenyang

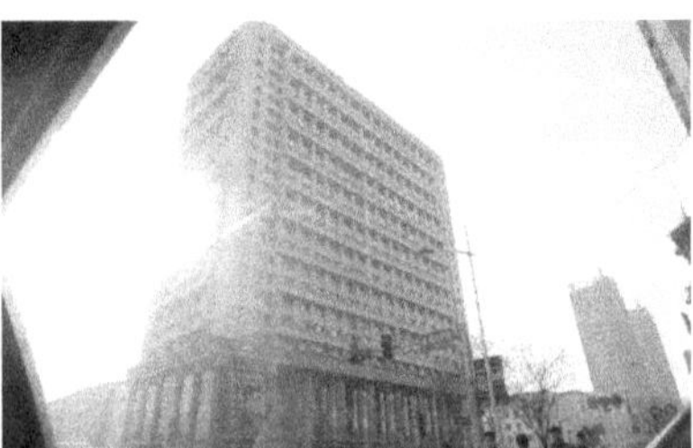

A building in Shenyang

A suburb in Shenyang

A street in Shenyang

SHAANXI

A region with 37 million residents, China's central province of Shaanxi is regarded as one of the cradles of Chinese civilization. It served as capital for thirteen feudal dynasties (Zhou Dynasty to the Tang Dynasty) in a space of about 1,100 years.

Shaanxi borders the provinces of Henan in the east, Chongqing in the south, Gansu in the west and Inner Mongolia in the north. The province has a well-developed tourism industry with numerous historic cultural sites, including 72 imperial mausoleums which are popular attractions. In 2015, it had around 386 million visitors, generating $46 billion in revenue to the government. Popular attractions here include the famous Terra Cotta Warriors and Horses, the Huashan Mountain and the Hukou waterfall on the Yellow river. Folk culture such as traditional Chinese paper cutting is also a puller.

Shaanxi is a mineral-rich region with vast reserves for coal, petroleum, natural gas and nonferrous metals estimated to be worth more than $ 6.4 trillion. The province is also a growing education hub with 108 colleges. Over 300,000 students from China and overseas graduate from universities in Shaanxi every year.

This is one of the provinces that showcases how investment in infrastructure and connectivity can transform a region. The vastly mountainous region is surprisingly very interconnected with a paved road network of over 5,000km and railway network of over 4,900km, linking it to neighbouring provinces and major cities. A high-speed railway network connects Shaanxi to the north, middle and southern parts of the region. Shaanxi is now home to five airports (both military and civilian flights), with connections to 185 cities both at home and abroad. In 2015, the province had a GDP of $280 billion, ranking 16th in China. A growing science and technological hub today, Shaanxi also has a large industrial base in the fields of aviation, aerospace and weaponry.

Xian City

In the ancient times Xi'an was regarded as one of the four major civilized ancient capitals in the world. Xi'an used to be the center of politics, economy and culture of ancient China.

The city's numerous attractions highlight its ancient glory and modern tastes. The Bell Tower of Xian, the largest and best-preserved of its kind in China, stands tall in the heart of the city, surrounded by upscale malls and fashion houses. Then, there is the famous X'ian City Wall, the most complete city wall that served as an ancient military defensive system, yet today it draws peace-loving tourists. Xian City has changed in many ways from its ancient past but its history remains intact. Decent public transport systems have left the city vastly interconnected. The people we met in Xian are full of life. In the evenings, young people throng public squares to play karaoke or just hang out with friends.

Emperor Qinshihuang's Mausoleum Site Museum

We travel up to the northern foot of Lishan Mountain to the Qinshihuang Mausoleum, the tomb of Emperor Qinshihuang, founder of the first unified empire in Chinese history during the 3rd century BCE.

It is the most famous landmark in Xian and the entire Shaaxi province. Standing tall in different sections of the site are thousands of life-size terracotta soldiers, terra cotta horses and bronze chariots and weapons. The statues would never have been discovered had it not been for farmers who stumbled across the archeological site in 1974.

Afraid of death, Emperor Qin is said to have ordered work on the mausoleum soon after he ascended the throne in 246 BC at the age of 13. The army would protect and serve him in the after-life. Early accounts indicate that full-scale construction started after he had conquered states and unified China. It is believed that it took 38 years (246 to 208 BC) to complete the project.

No two terracotta warriors or horses bear the same features, a reflection of the advances in pottery, chariot assembly, metallurgy and metal processing in the Qin Dynasty. Emperor Qin Shi Huang's unification drive was not only about territory but also creating a single system of writing, money, weights and measurement.

The tomb of Emperor Qinshihuang is the largest in Chinese history and features a large collection of objects that offer insight into the unprecedented political, military and economic power, as well as the advanced social, cultural and artistic level of the empire.

The range of unearthed tools such as lances, swords, axes, halberds, bows and arrows bear testimony to the level of military organization in China. The mausoleum of Qin Shi Huang is the largest preserved site in China. Inside some sections of the site, archeologists are still at work, taking measurements and preparing to uncover more ancient finds. The terracotta museum draws thousands of tourists every day.

Xi'an Culinary Street

We come across the famous Xian Culinary Street, an alley filled with rows and rows of food marts. From stir-fry lamb to spices, roast walnuts and prunes, vendors sell food of all taste.

Food tourism is a big attraction in this part of Xi'an. There are hundreds of tourists passing you by at any one moment. There are many Muslims around one corner, selling a variety of sauces and soups.

At one end a trader prepares noodles with a different kind of touch. He stretches out the dough order so long that it could reach the next vendor a few metres away. Xi'an is clearly a food city and a couple of restaurants are spread all over, offering both ancient-style delicacies and western cuisines.

Xi'an Port

Xi'an has grown into a modern city. We visit one of the industrial parks, the Xi'an International Trade and Logistic Park. It is the largest comprehensive logistics park in western China and a logistics center of product delivery, freight distribution, and container shipment connecting western China with the world. That helps link northern China to much of the Asia sub region. Inside the 44.6 square-kilometre area, efficient transportation systems have been established to cater for water, air, railways and road transport. Businesses that transact inside the park enjoy lower logistics costs and access to government services.

Yan'an City

It is hard to believe what you find in an area surrounded by so many mountains. The last thing you would expect to find is a modern city carved out of nowhere. This is Yan'an, a city located in the northern part of Shaanxi Province. The city has a long history stretching back about 1,400 years as a political, economic, cultural and military center.

During World War II, rural outposts in Yan'an served as headquarters for Chinese anti-Japanese troops and partners, including the US. Many buildings were bombed, forcing many people to retreat to cave-like dwellings carved into hillsides, known as 'yaodongs.'

Yan'an is somewhat a pilgrimage site for believers in the Communist philosophy, having been the birthplace of the revolution that ushered the Communist Party of China into power. The famous Long March, a perilous trek by Communist forces led by Mao Zedong and Zhou Enlai to escape from invading Kuomintang forces, is traced to this area. They lived there for 13 years. It is this place that consolidated the position of Mao as a leader. He wrote a lot and published 112 essays from this place.

We take a tour around the Jujube Garden that attempts to recreate the journey Mao Zedong, Zhou Enlai and communist troops took to fight against the Kuomintang. Not far away from this site is the Yan'an Revolution Memorial Hall, an imposing museum built to commemorate the Communist Party's arduous journey across rural villages with barely enough to eat or boast about. Today, Yan'an, a city of about 2.1 million inhabitants, is changing fast. Upscale shopping malls, hotels and apartments have sprouted across different corners of the central business area. There is such a huge network of expressways cutting through mountains to connect Yan'an to the coastal cities and provinces. The pace of construction is fast. A vast network of bridges and flyovers are coming up and new streets are emerging from a seemingly desolate landscape, along with rows of trees. In the next few years the city will be very different.

Our last stop in Yan'an is in Liangjiahe village. During the Cultural Revolution, an attempt to clean the country of capitalist and traditionalist ideas saw many urban-bred Chinese sent to remote villages for some form of 're-orientation.' Many remote villages in Yan'an received dozens of youth. One of the young men sent to Yan'an was none other than the current Chinese President, Xi Jinping, who was 15 years old at the time. The future leader would spend seven years in Liangjiahe village. Cast from the frills of privilege into the life of peasants, Xi had to adapt to difficult living conditions in the rural countryside. He was ushered into a small, cave-like apartment carved out of a hillside. Along with several young men, he would be taught how to work on the farm, cook and live a simple lifestyle based on the ideals of communism. In personal notes pasted on the walls of the 'apartment,' some local residents describe Xi as an honest and visionary boy. He organized the setting up of the first biogas plant and, many years later, pushed to have the village connected to the power grid.

A few of the books he read still lie in the room as exhibits, ranging from literary texts to books on Communism. So are some of his beddings, utensils and suitcase.

The son of revolutionary veteran Xi Zhongxun (one of the founding fathers of the Communist Party), Xi would rise to become one of China's leaders. Not surprising that in his journey of leadership, Xi has been a champion of rural development and architect of the Chinese Dream to see everyone prosperous.

XIAN CITY ▸▸

Life-size statues of warriors

A section of the Ancient Xian City Wall

A street in Xian City

XIAN CULINARY STREET ▸▸

YANAN CITY ▸▸

An extensive road network in Yanan City, Shaanxi Province

LIANGJIAHE VILLAGE ▸▸

Liangjiahe Village in Yanan City where many Chinese youth, including President Xi Jinping were sent on an orientation program in the 1960s. The village was an important base for fighters during the anti-Japanese movement and the war that brought the communist party of China into power in 1949. The village is now a popular tourist destination

116

FUJIAN

Our last trip outside Beijing leads us to Fujian, a province located on the southeast coast of the Chinese mainland, close to Taiwan. In this region of about 39 million people, man and nature tamed each other, transforming important landscapes into vibrant economic hubs. Fujian is the starting point of the ancient Maritime Silk Road. With an extensive coastline extending 6,128 km and over 120 natural harbors, the region has grown over the years into an important trade and tourism nerve.

Fujian is also a major hometown for many Chinese in the diaspora. At least 15.8 million Chinese living abroad have their roots there, including more than a million living in Hong Kong and Macau, as well as 80% of Taiwanese. Fujian was one of the two pioneer provinces to open up to the outside world. Now, it is a pilot area for China's comprehensive reform and opening up drive. It has a highly export-oriented economy and a well-developed market characterized by a dynamic private sector.

For the last 30 years of the reform and opening up policy, great changes have come to a region once heavily underdeveloped economically and socially. Today, it is regarded one of the most vibrant economies in China with the fastest growth rate. In 2015, its GDP totaled $414.37 billion and with per capita GDP of $10,680.

Heavy investment in infrastructure in Fujian is easily noticeable. With some 3,300 km of railway lines, 5,000 km of expressways, 413 million tons of cargo traffic at ports and 38 million passenger travels through airports in Fujian, the region is on the rise. And for this, the province is now a modern industrial hub with a large profile of industries in electronic information, machine building, petrochemicals, and science and technological innovation.

Even in the face of rapid growth, Fujian has placed protection of the eco-system and natural environment at the heart of development. The region ranks among the top in China in terms of air and water quality. The province has established trade ties with 223 countries and regions in the world, as well as twinning pacts with cities in 36 countries. So, what exactly do you find in Fujian?

Xiamen City

Our first stop is Xiamen, a city of about 3.9 million residents that directly faces Taiwan, a self-governing state that China claims to be part of its territory. Xiamen is regarded as one of the most competitive economies of China. In this was China's first special economic zone set up in 1980 initially covering a land area of 2.5 square kilometres. Today, the entire city is a special economic zone and a model of development and economic reform. The city's journey of economic and market reform is chronicled at the Xiamen Planning and Exhibition Hall, where artistic impressions and designs detail what Xiamen city will look like in the next few years, with futuristic towns and planned residential and economic hubs. So how will they do it?

We head to the Xiamen Pilot Free Trade Zone, home to dozens of foreign and local enterprises that enjoy preferential policies, such as tax exemption and business registration. Here, it takes five minutes to complete an online application for a business license. And if all desired documents are submitted, an individual or firm is guaranteed to receive their license that very day.

Set up in 2015, the free trade zone had by that year generated $22.8 billion from services, industry, shipping and logistics. About 25 government agencies have settled at the free trade zone, cutting the time it takes for each agency to verify papers from 30 days 20 years ago, to just hours today. The market reforms have boosted Xiamen's trade and growth of modern ports and logistics centres that have changed Xiamen from a rural countryside to a thriving modern city.

In a larger geopolitical sphere, the city serves more than just a commercial role. Its proximity to Taiwan grants Xiamen a strategic position in China's ties with the self-governing island. Several enterprises from across the strait have set in Xiamen, giving rise to joint investment, technology and processing zones. The city's revenues have been growing. In 2015, the regional GDP in Xiamen reached $50.7b, at 7.2% growth.

Xiamen is arguably the most livable city in China, known for its refreshing picturesque landscape, a city that former US president Richard Nixon once described as "China's coziest city".

It is home to numerous tourist attractions. We visit Gulang Islet, also called the "Piano Islet", a popular tourist destination. The name

Gulang (drumming wave) is drawn from a story of a rock in one part of the islet that sounded like a drum each time the raging waters hit it. Not far away is the Jinmen Island, currently administrated by Taiwan. It is the closest peek one gets into some of the framework of coexistence between the mainland and Taiwan.

Gulang draws thousands of tourists from across the strait every day. After the Opium War in 1842, at least 13 countries including Britain, USA, France, Japan, Germany, Spain and Holland set up their consulates in the area. Some of houses and villas that bear Western designs have been kept intact. Around Gulang Islet, some tourists perch up on a rock next to the statue of Zheng Chenggong, a famous Chinese general who resisted the Qing Dynasty conquest of the area. For some visitors, their only attraction is just to enjoy the pristine views of the vast waters near Shuzhuang Garden, an elegant sea-side park initially built as a private garden in 1931.

Domestic tourism is big in China. In the past, traffic to this part of Fujian was one-way (from the mainland to Taiwan), which was much more developed. Today, some people in Taiwan want to visit different spots. Development has become an attraction. So too have the shared history and culture.

Zhangzhou city

An hour's ride on a bus leads us to the city of Zhangzhou, nestled in the southeastern corner of Fujian, also facing the Taiwan Strait. It has as many as five million inhabitants.

Our first stop is at the Double Happiness Island, an artificially expanded island inside an economic and technological development zone. The artificial island offers insight into an integrated development model that takes into account protection of the environment, transport, industry and services, with the purpose of creating a harmonious living environment.

The same model has spread across China, unlike many years ago when what appeared to be the main driver was the speed to develop. In this island will be clusters of advanced industries, modern housing apartments, a decent transport network and green public spaces. Clusters of industries focusing on education and culture, tourism, entertainment and technology will all be housed in this hub, complete with customs, inspection and quarantine services. The transformation is thus: from a laid-back coastal region many years ago into a world-class satellite town. Work on this hub has already started and several local and foreign firms have already bought into the project.

Fujian is known to be an agricultural region but some of the things that grow in Zhangzhou are surprising. And surprise is what you find at the Zhangzhou Botanical and Agricultural Demonstration Park, where flowers and botanical plants take on new meaning. Modern farming methods are on show inside the expansive exhibition hall. The modern agricultural park is a repository of subtle practices that demystify agriculture as a 'dirty' occupation.

But the park is more than just a demonstration zone: it is one of the pilot zones that serve as a bridge between the two sides of the strait. Every year, there is a joint exhibition held here that brings together enthusiasts from both the mainland and Taiwan. Besides agriculture, industrialization in Zhangzhou is gathering pace, with the city now home to advanced industries including petrochemicals, special steel, equipment manufacturing and food, along with emerging industries of electronic information, new material, new energy and biomedicine.

Quanzhou City

Our journey into Fujian leads us to the city of Quanzhou, southeast of Fujian. Quanzhou was the largest port in Asia during the Song Dynasty (960-1279) and Yuan Dynasty (1271-1368). Famous explorers Marco Polo and Ibn Battuta are said to have visited Quanzhou and praised it as one of the most glorious cities in the world.

Quanzhou is considered the starting point of the Maritime Silk Road, a strategic initiative to increase investment and foster collaboration across China's ancient trade route. Early accounts indicate that thousands of merchants, missionaries, envoys, nobles and civilians from Asia, Africa and Europe met in Quanzhou. So did the different religions including Islam, Catholicism, Judaism and Hinduism.

Some of the relics of the era are exhibited at the Quanzhou Maritime Museum. Stone cuttings dating back to the Yuan Dynasty and early Ming Dynasty have been discovered in Quanzhou, which is now an important cultural and tourism destination. The city is widely regarded as the centerpiece of early encounters between Chinese and Western civilizations. For instance, some of the relics such as stone carvings bear symbols with elements of different religions or text written in multiple languages such as Persian, Latin, English and Chinese.

The ancient-style structures and remains of Song Dynasty ships showcase Quanzhou's fascinating maritime past. So are collections of historical gravestones carved to commemorate the death of foreign merchants from various cultures and religions living in Quanzhou more than a thousand years ago. Today, Quanzhou is a thriving coastal city connected by a network of high-speed trains and expressways linking to neighbouring cities such as Fuzhou, Xiamen and Zhangzhou.

Fuzhou City

Our last stop in this region is Fuzhou, the capital city of Fujian province. Fuzhou is one of the first 14 port cities to be opened during the reform and opening up.

The model of reform here is no different from what we have seen in other parts of the province – the idea of creating pilot zones through which modernization spreads out. One such area is the Fuzhou Binhai Industrial Area established in July 2002. The planned area covers 92 square-kilometres, with a cluster of planned industries along the coastline dealing in tourism, resorts, culture and entertainment.

Part of the area consists of three zones: residential zone, tourism zone and coastal industrial park, sitting on an area of 31 square-kilometres. Such is the ambition to transform an erstwhile underdeveloped suburb into a smart city. And speed is evidently a driver. Fuzhou is a well-connected city served by road, railway and marine transport.

Just when it appears we have seen enough of this city, we are introduced to one other important attraction: the Three Lanes and Seven Alleys, an ancient city landmark dating back to the Tang and Song Dynasties. Located in the city center and covering an area of 40 hectares, the centuries-old neighborhood comprises of former residences of historic celebrities and ancient architectural style of the dynasty era, featuring flagstone paths, white walls, black tiles and art. The apartments reflect the ancient style and culture of that time.

Pingtan Island

We wind up our trip of Fujian in Pingtan, the fifth largest island in China that covers 392 square-kilometres and home to 430,000 residents. The island sits on the west side of the Taiwan Straits. It lies barely 68 miles away from Xinzhu of Taiwan and is the closest area to Taiwan Island from Chinese mainland. Pingtan's strategic role in building relations between Taiwan and the mainland cannot be stressed enough. Here, the island enjoys provincial-level authority to make economic decisions.

And in July 2011, the Pingtan Comprehensive Pilot Zone was set up to become the largest special customs supervision area in China, with preferential policies to attract investment from both the mainland and Taiwan. Subsequently, in April 2015, a Pilot Free Trade Zone was officially launched. It means investors seeking to set up shop here are insulated from some taxes and bureaucratic procedures.

Within five years, the profile of investments on the island exceeded $21 billion, with revenue for 2015 reaching $2.7 billion. Today, Pingtan is being designed as an International Tourism Island. By 2020, the area will be teeming with clusters of advanced industries.

In Pingtan, heavy investments have been sunk into infrastructure to boost communication between mainland China and Taiwan. One such facility is the Aoqian Pier, through which passengers travel to and from Taiwan daily along two direct maritime routes. One route links Pingtan to Taibei and another to Taizhong.

It's time to leave Fujian, a land of sharp contrasts, rich culture, long history and fascinating sights. Many of the people who grew up in this area have many stories to tell. One such native is Ambassador Lin Songtian, the Director General of African Affairs, who is proud of the area's transformation in the past three decades.

XIAMEN ►►

Lin Songtian, a senior diplomat and native of Fujian has seen the Province grow since the late 1970s.

Xiamen is a decent city

Tourists come from as far as Taiwan, Macau and Hongkong

ZHANGZHOU ►►

Flowers and botanical plants at this park take on new meaning

Modern methods of agriculture on showcase at the Zhangzhou park

QUANZHOU ▸▸

A boat said to be a relic of the Maritime Silk Road era at the Quanzhou Maritime Museum

Quanzhou is a modern city

Quanzhou is a well-sculpted city

FUZHOU ▸▸

Students practice Wingchun inside th Three Lanes and Seven Alleys

Three Lanes and Seven Alleys, a famous tourist site in Fuzhou

BEIJING

W hat do you find in Beijing, the capital of the People's Republic of China? I have hailed a taxi, travelled by subway and walked about on the streets of this bustling city.

I spent much of my time in China in Beijing and lived through all the four seasons (winter, spring, summer and autumn), each season bringing forth a unique experience.

Beijing is the second largest Chinese city by urban population (22 million people), after Shanghai (24 million). It is China's political, cultural, and educational nerve centre.

This massive metropolis is one of the 'Four Great Ancient Capitals of China' (others are Nanjing, Luoyang and Xi'an) over the past eight centuries. The city bears hallmarks of China's ancient past as well as modern infrastructure. There are dozens of magnificent palaces, temples, parks, gardens and gates that showcase Beijing as a centre of culture and art in China.

The city's traditional housing style and narrow streets or alleys known as 'hutongs' are common in urban Beijing. The central business district features an ever-changing skyline filled with columns of space-hugging skyscrapers.

Home to the headquarters of most of China's largest state-owned companies, Beijing is also a major hub for the national highway, expressway, railway, and high-speed rail networks. Parts of Beijing such as Zhongguancun are thriving centres of innovation and technology.

Beijing is undeniably a place of diverse cultures. There is a large expat community here, especially in the urban districts such of Chaoyang, Dongcheng and Shunyi. People come here from all walks of life, some in search of opportunities and others in pursuit of leisure. It is a city littered with so many landmarks. Talk of the Great Wall or the Forbidden Palace, both of which we have visited. Beijing is a blend of an ancient past with modern tastes and traditions. It is a very cosmopolitan city too. You are sure to bump into people of all races across any street. Municipal authorities and organisations hold many events to keep the harmony and spread diversity.

A city on the move but also a place of reflection. That's Beijing for you. Dozens of theatres and entertainment spots are spread all over. So are quiet places, green parks and public squares. Walking is a popular mode of transport as much as it is a pastime for many. Decent public transport platforms are within walking distance, like the expansive Beijing Subway network. Electric buses, green and yellow taxis are on tap at every corner.

Many people here use electric bikes but cycling on conventional bicycles is still a norm. In the past, Beijing was known as the 'Bicycle

Kingdom of the World'. In many ways, the city is still a bicycle kingdom. Bicycle-sharing is big business and tech companies are trying to keep the age-old tradition alive. The number and shape of cars that drive on the roads is what you expect from a country that produces many of the popular brands.

Beijing is a fast-growing city. In fact, so fast that some of the city's administrative functions will have to be moved to the eastern district of Tongzhou. This relocation of services is part of a long-term integrated development plan meant to ease pressure on Beijing by developing outlying areas as far as Tianjin and Hebei province.

Located about 22km from central Beijing, Tongzhou has some iconic landmarks, including Yunhe Canal which stretches as far as Hangzhou in Zhejiang Province. In the past, it would take residents four hours by bus to get to downtown Beijing. Now, it takes about 40 minutes since the suburb is now connected to the Beijing Subway.

BEIJING »

A view of Beijing

Beijing is a cosmopolitan city with a large expat community

Tiananmen Square

Visitors at the Forbidden Palace in Beijing

The writer inside the Forbidden Palace

A section of the Great Wall in Beijing

Police at the opening of the 'Two Sessions'

International Kite Festival

TONGZHOU DISTRICT ▸▸

Tongzhou, which will be home to new Beijing administration offices

Yunhe Canal in Tongzhou

A contemporary dance show

Beijing rush hour

Chinese Opera is one of the attractions in Beijing

The writer at the Great Wall

An expressway in Beijing

One of the streets in Beijing

Decent road network in Beijing

Walkways and cycling lanes are wellgazetted

REFLECTIONS

Development is, above all, a way of thinking. It cannot, therefore, be easily identified with a particular strategy or programme, but ties many different practices and aspirations to a common set of assumptions. – **Wolfang Sachs**

China is a place that defies expectations. It is a land where centuries-old traditions are still strong and alive. A place where water, wind and fire mean much more than matter.

I have visited so many ancient sites mythologized in poetry, song and drama. I have been to the big cities and seen how the small rural towns are fast-changing. Many outbacks of China's pre-reform era are now thriving metropolises, carved out of difficult terrain through hard work and determination.

Poverty rates have fallen sharply and many young Chinese are living a life their parents only dreamt of. I have been to some arid regions in the far countryside that are turning into forests. In one generation, the country has grown from being poor to the world's second largest economy.

China lifted 660 million people out of poverty between 1978 and 2010, according to the 2016 China National Human Development Report. The country's development experience over the last 30 years has been described as nothing less than a "miracle", except that nothing here appears to have occurred by coincidence. Instead, it is clear the transformation has been a result of hard work.

But the job is not done yet. China still has an estimated 55 million people living below the poverty line, for whom the government has set a 2020 target to uplift. The East Asian nation still faces some challenges, including on the environment front, arising from both natural and manmade conditions.

Some economists believe that China offers an alternative development model to the developing world, one that focuses more on economic rights than on political rights. If there is one thing the country has demonstrated, it is that development is no longer about a particular system but the actual building blocks that matter. Liberal democracy and private capitalism propelled the US and western Europe to economic prosperity. China has built its wealth around a different model they prefer to call 'Sinified Socialism.'

Like the country's former leader Deng Xiaoping once stated: "It doesn't matter if a cat is black or white, as long as it catches mice." Under his leadership, China took a risk and opened its doors to private foreign investment but kept her guard. Conglomerates brought with them capital, skills and technology, which many state-owned and private enterprises harnessed and refined over the years.

The country has poured huge resources into infrastructure in the last three decades and has created an unmatched network of highways, ports and railways, linking underserved regions to big cities. Heavy investments in agricultural modernization, social security, environment and education are equally bearing fruit. Today, one in four engineers in the world is Chinese.

China, like her East Asian neighbours Japan and South Korea, has also risen to the top because of a strong work culture that embraces speed, consistency and strong leadership. The ambition to succeed is unimaginable, yet the values of discipline, respect for seniority (and authority), self-sacrifice and frugality are etched in the lives of the people.

Chinese people did not rely on foreign aid to develop; instead they tapped into the resolve and determination of leaders, the sacrifice of its people-home and overseas-and native innovations.

Different historical episodes have shaped Chinese thinking and choices. Before the 1970s, China, a nation surrounded by much smaller but richer neighbours, grappled with how to feed her people and defend herself. The country has come out of seemingly insurmountable odds and now sits at the table of the world's decision-makers. Whatever happens in China today can be felt anywhere across the world.

Africa could borrow a leaf from China's development experience. Many countries on the continent had far better economic indicators than China's in the early 1970s. Nigeria, Africa's largest economy, had a GDP per capita of $401, more than twice that of China ($158). Today, China, whose population exceeds that of Africa and the US combined, has a GDP per capita of $8,000, three times that of Nigeria ($2,600).

There are great stories about 'Africa Rising' and the push for a united and prosperous Africa is growing stronger. On account of growing economic and diplomatic ties many countries are turning to China to learn from her development experience. Like Zambian-born international economist and author, Dambisa Moyo suggests, Africa 'might have to tear those books up and start to look at other options' to chart a new development path."

On account of growing economic and diplomatic ties many countries are turning to China to learn from her development experience. First, they may have to re-examine the very assumptions on which they have hinged their development promises for the past generation or more. Then, like Zambian-born international economist and author Dambisa Moyo says: "We might have to tear those books up and start to look at other options and be open-minded to seek the truth."

Today, China is Africa's largest trading partner, with trade volumes of about $300b by 2017, and one of Africa's largest alternative sources of foreign direct investment. In recent years, more African countries are turning to China for more than just funding support but also lessons on development.

I lost count of the number of delegations from Africa we met in different Chinese cities and provinces on 'benchmarking' tours. If only they could bring back half the lessons.

A delegation of ambassadors from Africa at the Xiamen Pilot Free Trade Zone in Fujian Province

A delegation of Members of Parliament from Uganda at a Business Forum in Shenyang

A group of ministers from Africa at the Suzhou Industrial Park in Suzhou, Zhejiang Province

SITES & TREASURES

The 'Little Cars' of Beijing

Celebrating the arrival of spring in style

A robot at an International Fair in Beijing. China is investing more in science and technology

Flowers of Spring

Sunday service in Beijing

The writer and a friend at the Qingming Festival in Beijing

The writer at a press briefing inside the Great Hall of the People